AVE *with*
AMIE

SAVE with

JAMIE

HarperCollins*Publishers*Ltd

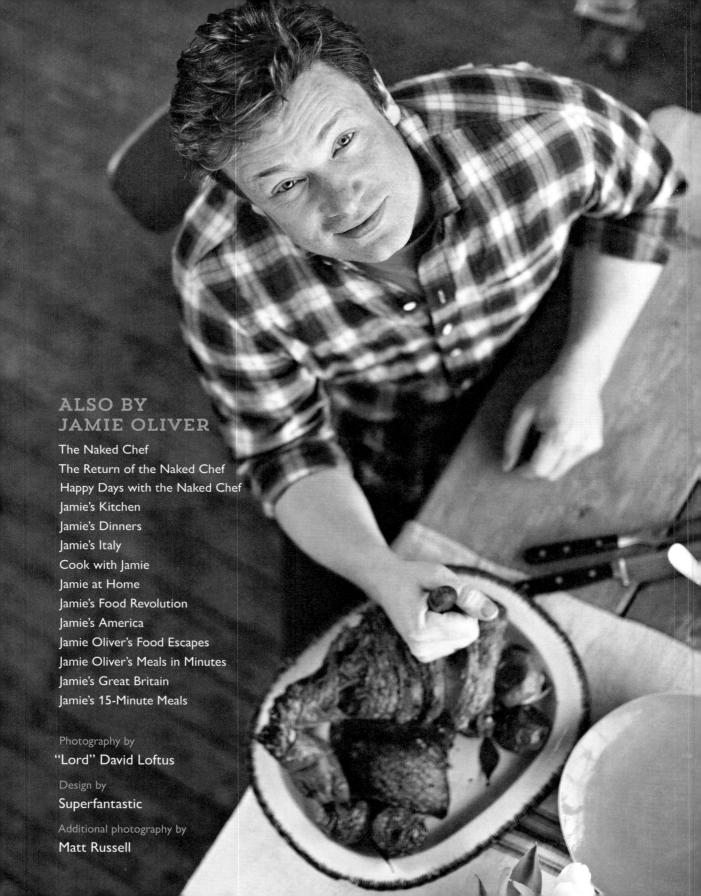

ALSO BY JAMIE OLIVER

The Naked Chef
The Return of the Naked Chef
Happy Days with the Naked Chef
Jamie's Kitchen
Jamie's Dinners
Jamie's Italy
Cook with Jamie
Jamie at Home
Jamie's Food Revolution
Jamie's America
Jamie Oliver's Food Escapes
Jamie Oliver's Meals in Minutes
Jamie's Great Britain
Jamie's 15-Minute Meals

Photography by
"Lord" David Loftus

Design by
Superfantastic

Additional photography by
Matt Russell

Save with Jamie

Copyright © 2013 by Jamie Oliver. All rights reserved.
Photography © 2013 by Jamie Oliver Enterprises Limited.
All rights reserved.
Photography: David Loftus
and Matt Russell (pp. 3, 12, 20, 23, 77, 117, 155, 177, 193, 217)

Published by HarperCollins Publishers Ltd, by arrangement with Michael Joseph,
an imprint of Penguin Books

First Canadian edition

No part of this book may be used or reproduced in any manner whatsoever
without the prior written permission of the publisher, except in the case of
brief quotations embodied in reviews.

HarperCollins books may be purchased for educational, business, or sales
promotional use through our Special Markets Department.

HarperCollins Publishers Ltd
2 Bloor Street East, 20th Floor
Toronto, Ontario, Canada
M4W 1A8

www.harpercollins.ca

Library and Archives Canada Cataloguing in Publication
information is available upon request.

ISBN 978-1-44342-923-8

Printed in Italy by Graphicom
Color reproduction by Altaimage Ltd

9 8 7 6 5 4 3 2 1

www.jamieoliver.com

THIS BOOK IS DEDICATED TO . . .

. . . ALL THE AMAZING STAFF AND VOLUNTEERS AT JAMIE'S MINISTRY OF FOOD CENTERS UP AND DOWN THE UK, AND ALL THE GUYS INVOLVED IN MY FOUNDATION PROGRAMS IN THE UK, USA AND AUSTRALIA. EVERY ONE OF THEM WORKS HARD TO EMPOWER AND INSPIRE PEOPLE TO COOK TASTY, NUTRITIOUS FOOD FROM SCRATCH, AND TEACH THEM HOW TO NOURISH THEMSELVES AND THEIR FAMILIES IN ORDER TO LEAD HEALTHIER, LONGER LIVES. ULTIMATELY THAT'S WHAT THIS BOOK IS ALL ABOUT - HELPING PEOPLE TO SHOP SMART, COOK CLEVER AND WASTE LESS.

TO FIND OUT MORE ABOUT MY FOUNDATIONS, PLEASE CHECK OUT JAMIEOLIVER.COM/FOUNDATION.

CONTENTS

I'M LISTENING

Very simply, this book exists because you guys asked for it. Through your requests on jamieoliver.com, Twitter, Facebook and Instagram, the need for delicious, exciting food that's not hard on your wallet was very clear, so I've listened. And to be honest, when you, the public, focus me on a brief like *Save with Jamie*, although it involves an incredible amount of research, work and recipe testing, I absolutely love it. For years I've been telling people that if you look back through history, the best food in the world has always come from communities under massive financial pressure, but the proviso is that you *must* be able to cook! If you can't and have no money, that's when the trouble starts. So this book is very clear in its intention – ultimately it's here to help you eat well, and to:

shop smart • cook clever • waste less

This book is relevant to every household – whether you're a couple, a family, a houseful of students or living on your own, I guarantee you'll find recipes and principles that you can use every day. It's a celebration of big, exciting flavors, and the array of delicious dishes is naturally inspired by many countries around the world. But, most importantly, every recipe is really accessible, trustworthy and, above all, super affordable. Each meal will easily cost you less per person than an average fast-food takeout, and it's not about trading down, it's about being clever. Stats suggest that the average family in the US throws away roughly $1600 of food and drink a year – that's about $124 billion across the nation,* which is an insane amount of waste. Use this book the way it's intended and you'll waste less, as well as save a wodge of cash.

I've made sure the book is really easy to navigate, with six clear chapters: veg, chicken, beef, pork, lamb and fish. There's loads of advice on getting stocked up and making sure your kitchen has everything you need to cook from scratch, as well as plenty of tips on making the most of your ingredients, stretching them further and using bits up. It's also about encouraging you to shop around and shop wisely, using supermarkets, butchers, greengrocers, fishmongers and markets. This is where the book comes into its own, giving you the ability to keep people well fed, happy, nourished and healthy while keeping costs under control. I'm here to arm you with as much helpful information as possible.

We all need to understand the basics about food, where it comes from and how it affects our bodies, as well as the importance of good, tasty cooking. My nutrition team have worked closely with me on the book to ensure that there's clarity on each page with calorie information per portion, and there's lots of extra detail at the back (see pages 268–72), to help you make informed choices. I hope *Save with Jamie* serves you well, gives you beautiful, nutritious food and some great mealtime memories, with the reassurance that none of it will break the bank. A cookbook that from start to finish has delicious recipes, all dedicated to great value, is a brilliant weapon to have on the shelf, whoever you are. I hope it gets passed down through your family to your children – it will certainly be my kids' first cookbook when they're ready. Good luck and happy cooking.

THE
BIG FREEZE

A freezer is definitely a good cook's best friend. We need to forget about the days of freezers filled with processed food and remember that this technology is phenomenal for keeping and saving things, so you're wasting less, and you can easily store meals. Below is a list of what I always keep in mine. Geekily, I enjoy keeping it well organized, having a regular sort-out, and tend to be fairly logical about where things are stored. And of course, when you're using frozen stuff, it's easier to just use what you need. So get stocked up – without a doubt, when it comes to having flavor bombs and last-minute meals sitting in the freezer ready for a rainy day, you'll be glad of it.

I keep a lot of frozen veg – they're great value, nutritious, available all year, perfect for many types of cooking, and you can just grab a handful of what you need, when you need it:

- Peas, fava beans, spinach, cauliflower, green beans, broccoli, corn (on and off the cob)
- A note on mushrooms – whether it's ones you've picked or bought, they freeze pretty well – they lose a bit of texture but they're useful and give wonderful flavor

My top drawer is full of stuff for adding flavor, that freezes well and can be used easily from frozen:

- Chiles (see page 184) and gingerroot that are getting a bit sad
- Curry and bay leaves, and kaffir lime leaves if I've got them
- Ice-cube trays of picked or chopped fresh herbs, spices or garlic preserved in oil (see page 208) or dripping (see page 158) for starting off cooking
- Homemade pestos and curry pastes
- Bags or containers of leftover homemade broth

Bread and dough are great things to freeze:

- I always have packs of soft flour tortillas and pitas in there, as well as some quality sliced bread for toasting
- Roll out homemade dough into pizza bases, stack and freeze them, and do the same for flatbreads and rolls – shape, wrap and freeze – they'll come in really handy

Protein-wise I'm pretty standard:

- Frozen shrimp
- A mixture of fish that's bought frozen as fillets, or fresh on offer and frozen – oily fish freezes best texturally, but white fish is fine if you're popping it into pies, curries or stews
- A box of fish fingers (I like a bap once in a while!)
- Jools will often make things like fishcakes and fish pie and freeze extra for emergency meals for the kids

Leftover meals are great in the freezer. Get into the habit of boxing or bagging stuff up, by the portion, labeling it (to avoid freezer roulette!) and freezing for quick, easy meals.

On the sweet front you'll regularly find:

- Frozen fruit – always really useful (see page 266)
- Homemade ice lollies and sorbets (see page 266)

There are a few basic rules. Let food cool before freezing, but break it down into portions so it cools quicker and you can get it into the freezer within 2 hours of cooking. Make sure everything is well wrapped, meat and fish especially, and thaw in the fridge before using. Generally, if you've frozen cooked food, after you've reheated it, don't freeze it again.

CHILL OUT

Rather than giving you a big old list of what you must and mustn't have in your fridge on a regular basis, I thought it would be more helpful to give you an example of what my fridge looks like. As you can imagine, there's a million and one things going through there every day, but as far as staples that are always, always in there are concerned, I definitely have a standard list of stuff, a lot of which pops up time and again in this book. Here's an inventory of what I've got going on, to give you a bit of a guide. It's not a list of essentials, but hopefully a helpful place to start.

The top shelf and door of my fridge tend to contain an assortment of jars of all those condiments and bits and pieces that come in handy for everyday cooking:

- Pickles, gherkins, pickled onions and pickled chiles (see page 184), as well as anything I've jarred myself, like the mighty house pickle (see page 176)
- Sauces like ketchup, BBQ, hot chili and sweet chili
- Mustards – English, Dijon and grainy
- Any dripping I've saved from beautiful roast meats, which keeps happily in a jar for a few months (see page 158)
- Jars of different jams and marmalades

Fruit- and veg-wise I'll always have staples like carrots, onions, squash and leeks, as well as:

- A selection of seasonal greens
- Ginger and chiles (but if they're a few days old I'll move them to the top drawer of the freezer)

Always a standard array of salad items:

- Cucumber, scallions, radishes, and my favorite cheap salad leaf, the humble bibb lettuce (my lot love it)
- Lots of lemons and a couple of limes
- Fresh herbs, wrapped in damp paper towel (see page 208) – this applies to other delicate leaves too

No surprises on the dairy front:

- Butter – always unsalted
- A container of organic fat-free plain yogurt – great for breakfast, but also for dressings and dolloping over meals
- Usually a couple of nice cheeses, but for everyday use always a good block of sharp Cheddar, a piece of Parmesan and a package of feta (great used as a seasoning)
- Milk – reduced-fat (2%) for cooking, preferably organic
- Eggs – large, and preferably free-range or organic

Meat and fish varies with what's available at the butcher's or fishmonger's, but more often than not I'll have the following meat, always kept on the bottom shelf while raw:

- Bacon – always smoked
- Chicken thighs – Certified Humane as a minimum, but preferably pasture-raised or organic if you can afford it
- Quality ground meat comes in very handy

Drinks are always useful:

- A chilled bottle or pitcher of tap water
- Fresh fruit juices – not from concentrate
- Without question a bottle of wine and a few beers

Anything else that comes into the fray is what I'll randomly pick up to try, leftovers from the days before, or beautifully fresh seasonal produce, which obviously varies all year round.

STORE IT

I think the humble store cupboard or pantry is the most exciting place to be before you start cooking a meal. You can gather a collection of all kinds of wonderful things, whether dried, pickled, salted, jammed or fermented, and you're not going to waste anything because it's all just waiting for you, suspended and preserved in time, ready to inject a bit of magic into your cooking. Zone your spices, carbs, beans, oils and vinegars, condiments and so on in separate areas to make it easier for you to see and use them efficiently. Personally, I pull it all out maybe four times a year, have a spring clean, refresh some jars and bags, and make sure I'm not missing anything hidden at the back. There are definitely ways to save money in this area, and generally that means buying in bulk, or from a specific kind of retailer. So here's a taster of what I generally have in my pantry . . .

Staples for everyday cooking:

- Oils – olive, extra virgin, vegetable, peanut and Asian sesame
- Vinegars – white wine, red wine, cider, balsamic, malt and even a couple of homemade bottles (see page 70)
- Sea salt and freshly ground black pepper
- Bouillon cubes – a range of flavors and always organic
- Soy sauce – use a reduced-sodium version wherever possible

Spices and dried herbs – these are really useful for adding that all-important flavor. I regularly use smoked paprika, cumin, fennel seeds, ground coriander, dried oregano, cinnamon, turmeric (for great color), Chinese five-spice powder, whole cloves (for epic rice), nutmeg and garam masala, to name but a few. A jar of dried red chiles is always handy too (see page 184).

A range of nuts and seeds like pistachios, sliced almonds and sesame seeds – keep these fresh in well-sealed containers.

Pasta and noodles – buy big bags to get the cost down. At the end of each package, smash up the last of the pasta and keep it in an "odds and ends" jar for using in soups and stews. I always have spaghetti, penne, shells and whatever else takes my fancy. I keep rice and egg noodles in a variety of different thicknesses, as well as buckwheat, to mix it up a bit.

Rice, grains and pulses – big bags give you better value and can be easily stored in large jars. I always have basmati, brown, risotto and wild rice, plus couscous, bulgur, pearl barley, quinoa, quick-cooking polenta and fine-ground cornmeal.

Canned and jarred foods keep really well, so get stocked up; just remember that most jars need to move to the fridge once open, and if you don't use a whole can of something, decant the rest into a container before popping it into the fridge – never leave it in the can. I always keep:

- Cans of diced and plum tomatoes, and jars of passata
- A good mixture of canned beans and pulses like chickpeas, lentils, cannellini, kidney and black beans
- Canned or jarred anchovies
- Jars of olives with the pits
- Curry pastes – Patak's does a great range
- A range of pickles, condiments and sauces

Baking staples, like:

- Flour – plain, self-rising, bread and Tipo "00"
- Superfine sugar
- Sachets of active dry yeast

SHOP SMART

Here are some of my favorite tips from all our thrifty friends up and down the country, plus some hints and ideas I've picked up over the years of working in the food industry. This info is what we think will help you to save dramatic amounts of cash. A lot of it is common sense, but I think it's useful to get it all down in one easy-to-reference place – if you start following a few of these strategies, I'm sure it will have a really positive impact on your weekly shop, which, in turn, will make a big difference to your annual finances.

MAKE A SHOPPING LIST

That way you're more likely to stick to it. Go old-school with paper and pen, or keep a note on your phone, and make sure you check your fridge, freezer and cupboards before you shop – I know it sounds obvious, but that way you'll avoid doubling up and wasting things later.

THRIFTY!

If you're budgeting, go to a supermarket that price-matches so you can keep an eye on what you're spending. There are loads of helpful tools online, like mysupermarket.com, which will do the hard work for you, and online forums are another great place to pick up lots of tips from other thrifty shoppers. Get clued up before you head to the shops.

Menu planning is great, but don't let it restrict you. Flexi-planning is your best option – it will help you waste less, and means you won't get caught out if your plans change. Build in the option of embracing a few bits in the freezer for days you need last-minute meals. Look at offers before you shop, and see if you can shape any meals around them, but also embrace great-value seasonal produce wherever you can, backed up by your pantry staples. A bit of creativity while you're shopping, combined with some forethought before you set off, is what's going to serve you most well.

$AVE

Try shopping with cash only, and leaving your cards at home – that way, you'll be forced to think more about what you're buying and stick to whatever budget you set yourself.

Embrace **SEASONAL PRODUCE**

DON'T SHOP WHEN YOU'RE HUNGRY!

AN OLD CLASSIC

We've all done it, and if you're not careful you end up with a whole load of extra bits you don't really need, plus a snack for making your way round the supermarket.

Make sure you shop around

USE LOCAL SHOPS, GREENGROCERS, MARKETS, BUTCHERS, FISHMONGERS AND SUPERMARKETS.

Get to know your area and take advantage of where you'll be on different days, popping into different places as appropriate.

When you're at the supermarket, don't be tempted by things like buy-one-get-one-free schemes – remember, it's only a bargain if you need it or can genuinely use it. The one exception is if you see good-quality fresh meat or fish on offer, and you know you've got space to store it in the freezer. Pick it up while it's at a great price and ensure you freeze it asap.

Stock up on staples that have a long shelf life, such as rice, pasta, and dried and canned goods. Often you can buy these things in bulk, and if you've got the storage space, I think it's well worth it. If not, why not see if you can get together with friends or family, bulk buy, then share it out between you?

Using spices in your cooking adds tons of flavor, but I know some people worry about the cost of those little jars. Quite simply, buy them in big bags instead. You'll find them readily available in all ethnic stores, and a lot of supermarkets have started stocking the bags now too. They're a fraction of the price, and you get loads more for your money – simply decant them into airtight jars and label them; stored correctly, they'll last for ages.

Quality

Cash and carries are great for stocking up on basic ingredients you'll use every week, if you have access to them. You can pick up some great bulk buys, like cans of olive oil, sacks of rice and pasta, pallets of canned goods, big bags of frozen veg and much more, so if you've got the storage space or a chest freezer, you're laughing. Unfortunately you can't just walk in off the street, but get online to see which companies allow individual memberships – usually based on your profession – and take advantage of them, if you can, or ask a mate who does have access to split their wares with you.

PICK UP SOME REAL BARGAINS

A lot of supermarkets now have different policies on reducing goods that are nearing their sell-by date – get to know the times when products are discounted and take advantage of that if there are things you need, or shop at markets, as these almost always reduce their produce at the end of the day and you can pick up great bargains. A box of beautiful almost overripe tomatoes, for example, can easily be turned into passata, soup, sauce, or used in a delicious meal like my sausage panzanella (see page 180).

MIDNIGHT SECRETS

Find out more about what I like to call "midnight secrets." If you get yourself down to any of the large commercial markets for fruit and veg, fish and meat, in most of our big cities, you're likely to be able to pick up some brilliant bargains. This isn't about buying small scale, you will have to buy in bulk, but if you've got a decent chest freezer where you can store meat or fish, or if you can get together with family or friends, it can definitely help you out. There's a chance you'll be able to haggle on price and you're pretty much always going to need to pay with cash, but the advantage is that you're paying market rather than retail price. So if you want to pick up a whole large fish or a box of sardines, for example, give this a go – there's no restriction on the public going there, the only proviso is that you'll have to get up very early in the morning! There's already a fairly large group of both new and established immigrant communities shopping in this way and making the most of all these great bargains, so it's definitely something to think about.

WHAT YOU NEED

Good, basic kitchen equipment is widely available, so it's easy to get kitted out. Shop around to find the best prices and go for good-quality stuff where you can – it'll last much longer, perhaps even a lifetime. This list is what I think ensures you can cook great meals from scratch, plus a few extra gadgets to help you with speed and making things look their best.

Food processor	Box grater
Blender	Fine grater
Immersion blender	Mixing bowls
Large non-stick frying pan (12 inches)	Measuring cups
Medium non-stick frying pan (10 inches)	Measuring spoons
Small non-stick frying pan (8 inches)	Weighing scales
Grill pan (10 x 12 inches)	Colander
Large saucepan with lid (10 inches)	Fine sieve
Medium saucepan with lid (8 inches)	Pestle and mortar
Small saucepan with lid (6 inches)	Potato masher
Casserole pan with lid	Garlic press
Large sturdy roasting pan (12 x 14 inches)	Tongs
Non-stick baking sheets	Slotted spatula
12-cup muffin pan	Wooden spoon
12-cup shallow bun pan	Slotted spoon
Baking/lasagne dish (10 x 12 inches)	Ladle
Wooden cutting boards	Can opener
Plastic cutting boards	Rolling pin
Chef's knife	Pastry brush
Paring knife	Aluminum foil
Bread knife	Plastic wrap
Vegetable peeler (Y-peeler)	Parchment paper
Mandolin	Paper towels

The crinkle-cut knife is my gadget of choice at the moment. I'm loving it – you should get one! Pick one up online.

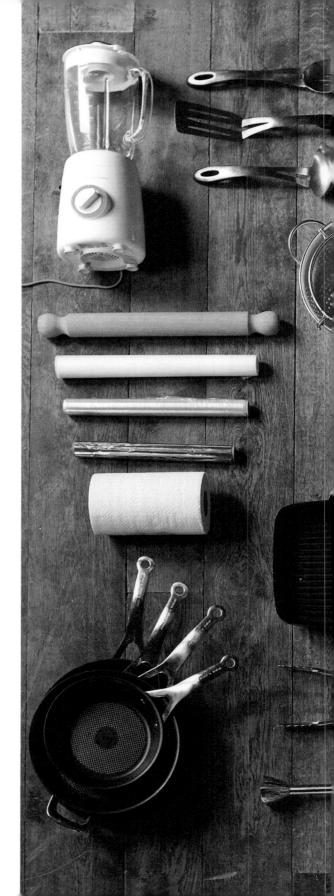

PORK

CHICKEN

Fish

LAMB

BEEF

Veg

• VEG RECIPES •

Colorful, exciting, vibrant, delicious dishes sing out on every page of this wonderful chapter, whether they're gorgeous complete meals or tasty side dishes. By no means did I want this to be just a vegetarian gesture, so in fact it's ended up being a bumper chapter, and the biggest one in the book. I think it's essential for everyone to aim to have two meat-free days a week – it's much healthier, will save you money and it helps to relieve the increasing pressure on meat farming. Above all, the biggest reason to eat a meat-free dish is because it's bloody delicious, and every single recipe in this chapter certainly delivers on that front. I have to say, some of my absolute favorites appear here – enjoy!

Grated rainbow salad
Sesame feta fritters

I was having a bit of fun when I made up this salad, and wasn't sure if I was in Greece or Morocco, but ultimately, the principle of a beautifully dressed salad with different textures and colors is always the same, regardless of the country you take it to. I'm a sucker for a crouton, so I wanted to try something different with pita here. I have to say, this mutt of a salad is very tasty and the sweet and savory sesame feta fritters are damn good.

Serves 4

Total time: 35 minutes

606 calories

1 mug (10 oz) of couscous

2 pita breads

olive oil

½ English cucumber

1 red onion

1 large carrot

3 ½ oz cooked or raw beets

3 ½ oz feta cheese

1 large egg

3 heaping tablespoons self-rising flour

1 heaping tablespoon raw sesame seeds

honey

2 tablespoons red wine vinegar

4 tablespoons extra virgin olive oil

1 teaspoon dried oregano

Preheat the oven to 350°F. Pop the couscous into a bowl, just cover with boiling water, then put a plate on top and leave for 10 minutes to do its thing. Slice the pitas ¼ inch thick, spread out evenly on a large baking sheet, drizzle lightly with olive oil and bake for around 10 minutes, or until golden, crisp and crunchy.

Meanwhile, coarsely grate the cucumber on a box grater, then peel and grate the onion, carrot and beets (you might want to wear rubber gloves to do this, and if using raw beets, peel them before you grate them). Mash the feta in a bowl with the egg, then mash in the flour. Place a large frying pan on a medium heat, add a lug of olive oil and dot in teaspoons of the mixture (you should get roughly 12). Cook until golden on the bottom, then scatter over the sesame seeds, pressing them in lightly before flipping the fritters over. Drizzle with honey and cook for a further 1 to 2 minutes, or until golden and sticky.

In a bowl, mix the vinegar, extra virgin olive oil, oregano and a pinch of salt and pepper together. Fluff up the couscous, season to perfection and tip onto a large platter, pile the grated veg on top and drizzle over the dressing, then toss everything together. Scatter over the crispy pita strips, arrange the sesame feta fritters on top and dig in.

Mexican filled omelet

I can't tell you how much I love these silky little omelets filled with Mexican-inspired deliciousness. Making and eating them is brilliant fun, and they're unusually fulfilling for a humble omelet. I've been making smooth avocado dressings for years, but never thought to use one to dress a slaw before – it's insanely good. Make these one by one, as your hungry guests sit by, watching and waiting for that little mouthful of heaven – they'll love you for it.

Serves 4
Total time: 20 to 25 minutes

355 calories

1 ripe avocado

3 limes

½ bunch of fresh cilantro (½ oz)

3 tablespoons fat-free plain yogurt

olive oil

1 small onion

1 carrot

½ head of white cabbage

1 fresh red chile

8 large eggs

2 oz Cheddar cheese

Squeeze the avocado flesh into a blender, discarding the pit and skin. Squeeze in all the juice from 2 limes, rip in the cilantro stalks, add the yogurt and a splash of oil and whiz until smooth, then season to perfection.

Peel the onion and carrot. Ideally in a food processor, or using a box grater and good knife skills, grate the onion and carrot, then finely slice the cabbage. Very finely slice the chile by hand, then tip everything into a large bowl. Add most of the cilantro leaves, then pour over the avocado dressing and toss together well. Taste and season to perfection again, if needed. Whisk all the eggs together in a bowl, with a splash of water to loosen and a pinch of salt and pepper.

Put a large non-stick frying pan on a medium-low heat. Once fairly hot, put in a tiny drizzle of oil followed by a quarter of the egg mixture. Swirl it all around the pan, grate over a quarter of the cheese and let it melt, then cook the omelet gently without coloring it, so it's soft, silky and smooth, for just under 2 minutes, only cooking on one side. Slide it onto a plate, spoon over a quarter of the avocado slaw, then gently fold up the sides and roll over. Serve with a wedge of lime and a few extra cilantro leaves. Repeat with the remaining ingredients, serving them up as you go.

Sicilian squash & chickpea stew

This is a delicious dish with great depth of flavor, gained from roasting the squash as well as stewing it, and also from the use of spices, which is common in many parts of Sicily. The island has been invaded and influenced from a culinary point of view several times, so you'll find some North African spices, dried fruit and even couscous, which are more usually associated with Morocco and Tunisia, being used very comfortably in Sicilian cooking.

Serves 4 to 6
Total time: 1 hour 25 minutes

547 calories

1 butternut squash (roughly 2 ½ lbs)

olive oil

2 onions

½ bunch of fresh cilantro (½ oz)

1 handful of raisins

1 teaspoon ground cinnamon

½–1 teaspoon dried chili flakes

1 handful of mixed olives, with pits

1 x 14-oz can of diced tomatoes

1 x 14-oz can of chickpeas

1 vegetable bouillon cube

1 mug (10 oz) of couscous

fat-free plain yogurt, to serve

Preheat the oven to 375°F. Peel the squash using a vegetable peeler, then carefully halve and seed it (put the strips of peel and seeds to one side in a bowl). Cut the squash into 1 ¼-inch chunks, place in a large roasting pan and toss with a little oil, then season lightly. Roast at the top of the oven for 35 to 40 minutes, or until golden and caramelized.

Meanwhile, peel and roughly chop the onions and put into a casserole pan on a low heat with a lug of oil. Finely slice the cilantro stalks and add to the pan, along with the raisins and most of the cinnamon and chili flakes. Cook for 20 minutes with the lid on, stirring occasionally and adding splashes of water, if needed. When the squash is done, stir it all into the casserole pan. Bash the olives and tear out the pits, then add the olives to the pan with the tomatoes and chickpeas (juice and all). Crumble in the bouillon cube, pour in 2 cups of boiling water, then turn the heat up to medium and simmer for 40 minutes (lid off), or until lovely and thick, stirring occasionally. Meanwhile, toss the reserved squash seeds and strips of peel with the remaining cinnamon and chili flakes and a pinch of salt and pepper, spread out in the empty roasting pan and roast for around 10 minutes, or until golden and crisp, then put aside.

Around 15 minutes before the stew is ready, pop the couscous into a bowl, just cover with boiling water, put a plate on top and leave for 10 minutes to do its thing. Fluff it up, season to perfection and tip onto a large platter. Spoon over the stew, and serve drizzled with yogurt, and scattered with the cilantro leaves and the scrunched-up squash peel and crispy seeds.

Puffy pea 'n' potato pie

I used to make something very similar to this, but in individual portions, as a vegetarian dish in my dad's pub in the '80s, so it brings back a lot of fond memories for me. It's based on the classic *petits pois à la Français*, which is the most delicious sweet pea, lettuce and onion dish, but I've added a few potatoes to bulk it up a bit, a little cottage cheese to lighten it, and made a family-style pie. This is a brilliant meat-free Monday dish.

Serves 6

Total time: 40 minutes

2 tablespoons all-purpose flour, plus extra for dusting

1 sheet ready-rolled puff pastry

1 large egg

1 onion

olive oil

1 large potato

3 ¼ cups frozen peas

1 large knob of unsalted butter

½ head of iceberg lettuce

1 vegetable bouillon cube

1 teaspoon English mustard

1 teaspoon mint sauce

4 heaping teaspoons cottage cheese

Preheat the oven to 400°F. On a flour-dusted surface, unfold the puff pastry (it should be roughly 10 x 15 inches), then transfer it to a large baking sheet. Score a 1 ¼-inch border onto the pastry (don't cut all the way through), then lightly score the inner section in a large criss-cross pattern. Beat the egg in a small bowl, then eggwash the whole thing. Bake for around 17 minutes, or until golden, risen and cooked through. Once done, remove from the oven and leave to one side to cool slightly. Using a sharp knife, lightly score round the border, cutting through the top few layers of pastry only, then use a slotted spatula to carefully lift up and remove the inner section (like a lid), leaving a layer of pastry at the bottom, and put to one side.

Meanwhile, peel and finely chop the onion, put it into a medium saucepan with a lug of oil and cook for around 10 minutes, or until soft and sticky, stirring occasionally. Peel the potato and cut into ½-inch dice, then stir into the pan along with the peas, butter and flour. Finely shred and add the lettuce, cook for another 10 minutes, then crumble in the bouillon cube and pour in 1 ¼ cups of boiling water. Bring to a boil, cover, and reduce to a simmer for 5 to 10 minutes, or until the potato is cooked through. Stir in the mustard and mint sauce, then season the mixture to perfection. Pour evenly into the pastry case, ripple through the cottage cheese, then carefully top with the pastry lid and serve in the middle of the table with a big salad.

Hungover noodles

This super-fast, super-tasty meal is perfect when you're feeling a little down or, let's be honest, a bit hungover, as it's full of the good stuff. Flavoring the noodles with a dressing is genius, and a runny fried egg on top is a bit of an added bonus. Drizzle with lots of chili sauce to ensure it gives you a slap around the face, and tuck in.

Serves 4

Total time: 20 minutes

537 calories

1 thumb-sized piece of gingerroot

1 clove garlic

2 tablespoons reduced-sodium soy sauce

3 tablespoons rice wine vinegar

3 tablespoons Asian sesame oil

1 head of Napa cabbage

1 lb fresh or frozen broccoli

8 oz medium egg noodles

7 oz snow peas

4 large eggs

olive oil

hot chili sauce, to serve

Peel the ginger and garlic and finely grate into a large bowl. Add the soy sauce, vinegar, sesame oil and a pinch of pepper, then mix to make a dressing. Trim and shred the cabbage and put it into a large saucepan of boiling salted water with the broccoli (cut into florets first, if using fresh) and noodles to cook for around 3 minutes, then add the snow peas for a final minute. Drain it all well, then toss in the bowl of dressing.

Meanwhile, fry the eggs in a large non-stick frying pan on a medium heat with a lug of olive oil until cooked to your liking (I like mine with a runny yolk). Divide the noodles between bowls, pop an egg on top of each one, and serve drizzled with chili sauce for that all-important added kick.

Using buckwheat noodles in this dish like the ones you see in the picture is really nice – they're a little bit more expensive but have a great flavor and texture. Just make sure you check the package instructions in case they take longer to cook. Feel free to chuck in any other fresh seasonal veg, or leftovers you have in the fridge.

Squash & spinach pasta rotolo

Rotolo is definitely one of the more unusual pasta dishes that you'll see – many people have never eaten it before. The way I've prepared mine means it kind of feels like eating a lasagne or a cannelloni, but it looks really pretty and you get the gnarly crispy bits of pasta on the top, complemented by the softer pasta hiding underneath the sauce.

Serves 4 to 6

Total time: 2 hours 20 minutes

430 calories

1 butternut squash (roughly 2 ½ lbs)

1 red onion

olive oil

1 teaspoon dried thyme

1 lb frozen spinach

1 whole nutmeg, for grating

4 cloves garlic

3 ¼ cups passata

6 large fresh pasta sheets
(roughly 6 x 8 inches each)

2 oz feta cheese

¾ oz Parmesan cheese

optional: a few sprigs of fresh sage

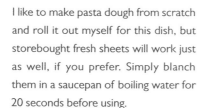

I like to make pasta dough from scratch and roll it out myself for this dish, but storebought fresh sheets will work just as well, if you prefer. Simply blanch them in a saucepan of boiling water for 20 seconds before using.

Preheat the oven to 350°F. Cook the squash whole in a roasting pan for around 1 hour 30 minutes, then remove from the oven. Meanwhile, peel and roughly chop the onion, put it into a medium saucepan on a medium-low heat with a lug of oil, the thyme and a pinch of salt and pepper, and cook for 10 minutes, stirring occasionally. Stir in the frozen spinach, cover with a lid and allow to slowly cook for another 15 minutes, or until the liquid has evaporated, then remove from the heat. Cut the squash in half, discard the seeds and skin, then mash up with a fork. Keeping them separate, season both the squash and spinach to perfection with salt, pepper and a grating of nutmeg.

Peel and finely slice the garlic, then put it into a shallow 11-inch casserole pan on a medium heat with a splash of oil and fry for a couple of minutes, or until lightly golden. Pour in the passata, then add a splash of water to the empty jar, swirl it around and pour it into the pan. Bring to a boil, simmer for just 3 minutes, then season to perfection.

On a clean work surface, lay out the pasta sheets facing lengthways away from you. Working quickly so your pasta doesn't dry out, brush them with water, then evenly divide and spread the squash over the sheets. Sprinkle over the cooked spinach and crumble over the feta. Roll up the sheets and cut each one into 4 chunks, then place side by side in the tomato sauce. Finely grate over the Parmesan, then pick the sage leaves (if using), toss in a little oil and scatter over the top. Bake for 35 to 40 minutes at the bottom of the oven until golden and crisp. Delicious served with a fresh green salad.

My sag aloo

Whenever I think about this dish my mouth starts to water. The sheer talent of our Indian brothers and sisters in the kitchen always blows me away — how can a simple dish taste so damn good? Have a go at this and you'll find out. Great-value, tasty food that's good as part of a curry, or even celebrated as a dish in its own right. Delish.

Serves 6

Total time: 50 minutes

234 calories

1 onion

2 ripe tomatoes

½ bunch of fresh cilantro (½ oz)

2 heaping tablespoons rogan josh curry
   paste

peanut oil

2 ½ lbs potatoes

4 cloves garlic

1 fresh red chile

2 teaspoons cumin seeds

10 oz frozen spinach

6 heaping teaspoons fat-free plain yogurt

Peel the onion and blitz with the tomatoes, cilantro stalks and curry paste in a food processor until combined, then spoon into a large non-stick frying pan on a medium heat with a lug of oil. Cook for 5 minutes, stirring regularly, while you cut the potatoes into 1 ¼-inch chunks (I like to leave the skin on — it saves a job and is more nutritious). Add them to the pan with a pinch of salt and pepper, then pour in enough water to come halfway up the potatoes but not cover them. Bring to a boil, pop the lid on or cover with aluminum foil, then simmer for 10 to 12 minutes, or until the potatoes are just cooked through. Remove the lid, then turn the heat up to medium-high and reduce until all the liquid cooks away and the potatoes start to get crispy and golden (around 15 to 20 minutes).

Meanwhile, to make the flavored oil (called a temper — this really brings the sag aloo to life), peel the garlic and finely slice with the chile, place in a small saucepan and fry with the cumin seeds and a good lug of oil until nicely golden, then take off the heat. When the potatoes are looking good, stir the spinach into the pan and cook down for around 5 minutes, or until the liquid has evaporated and the potatoes are nice and crisp, stirring regularly.

Serve the sag aloo drizzled with the temper, dolloped with yogurt, and with the cilantro leaves scattered on top. It's really delicious wrapped in soft bibb lettuce leaves with an ice-cold beer on the side.

Veggie korma
Mock cauliflower pilau

I always get very excited when I can create massive, delicious flavors in curries without using any meat, and as well as being good for you, it's good for your wallet too. To mix things up a bit, instead of using rice I've cooked cauliflower in such a way here that it looks, feels and acts like rice – it's really delicious. Have a go at this tasty recipe and I promise, even your most carnivorous all-man geezer mates will be happy.

Serves 4

Total time: 50 minutes

334 calories

1 heaping tablespoon sliced almonds

2 large sweet potatoes

olive oil

1 red onion

2 cloves garlic

1 thumb-sized piece of gingerroot

½ bunch of fresh cilantro (½ oz)

optional: ½–1 fresh red chile

1 handful of curry leaves

1 heaping tablespoon korma curry paste

1 x 14-oz can of chickpeas

1 large head of cauliflower

½–1 lemon

optional: 2 oz feta cheese

4 tablespoons fat-free plain yogurt

I've used storebought paste here, but to save even more pennies, why not try making your own?

Start by toasting the almonds in a large casserole pan until lightly golden, then tip out and set aside. Scrub the sweet potatoes clean, then cut into 1 ½-inch chunks and put them into the pan on a medium heat with a lug of oil. Fry for about 5 minutes, or until golden, while you peel the onion, garlic and ginger, then finely slice them with the cilantro stalks and chile (if using – it will give the sauce a real kick). Add the curry leaves to the pan and stir for 1 minute, then add all the sliced veg with the curry paste and cook for another 5 to 10 minutes, or until the onions have softened, stirring occasionally. Add the chickpeas (juice and all) with 2 ½ cups of boiling water, then bring everything to a boil. Reduce to a simmer and cook for around 30 minutes, or until thickened.

Meanwhile, break off and chop the cauliflower leaves, then finely slice the stalk and add both to the curry for the rest of the cooking time. Cut the florets into even-sized chunks and pulse in a food processor until they're the same texture and size as rice. Tip it into a microwave-safe dish and cover. Steam or microwave the cauliflower on high for 7 minutes, or until cooked through, just before serving.

Add a good squeeze of lemon juice to the curry, then season to perfection and crumble over the feta (if using – I think of it here as a nod towards Indian paneer, and it adds a lovely subtle bit of extra flavor). Dollop over the yogurt and stir it through for that korma creaminess (or serve on the side, if you prefer), then sprinkle with cilantro leaves and the toasted almonds. Tip the cauliflower onto a nice serving platter and dig in.

KNOW YOUR...
GREENGROCER

Supermarkets stock a fantastic range of fresh produce, and they absolutely serve a purpose, but it also pays to build up a good relationship with your greengrocer. They'll happily talk you through what's in season, when you can expect a glut or pick up a bargain, and you can buy exactly what you need. Here are some top tips from me and my greengrocer, John Leavey:

1 Always buy seasonally – it's the best produce at the best value. As John says: it's premium quality at the right price.

2 At a greengrocer's you can pick up small amounts of veg, meaning you can afford to get lots of variety into your dishes, which is much healthier as well.

3 Bulk buy veg where appropriate and store well – hardy veg like potatoes, squash and beets can all last a long time if stored properly. Potatoes with soil on, kept in brown paper bags in a dark place, will keep much better than those kept in a plastic bag in the fridge. And, if you're buying in bulk, it's going to be much cheaper per pound.

4 If you've got a budget for making a meal, tell your greengrocer what it is and they'll work hard for you.

5 Ask questions – if there's a vegetable you haven't seen or used before, get your greengrocer to give you some suggestions. Similarly, if a recipe gives you variations, ask your greengrocer what they'd recommend.

6 Most tradesmen want to get rid of stuff by the end of the day, so just before closing time is always when they'll start doing some good discounting. Keep your eyes peeled, ask questions, and you could be picking up stuff like big boxes of slightly too ripe tomatoes for next to nothing, which is good news for making passata, chutney, soups and sauces.

Tayshaw's, 60 Druid Street, Bermondsey, London, UK, SE1 2EZ

Sweet fennel soup
French toast croutons

I'm super pleased with this soup because it's big in flavor, it's ridiculously comforting and it's not your everyday predictable recipe. The play on French toast for the croutons, I think, makes total sense and means this dish is even more desirable, and to be honest, I can't believe I never thought of doing it before. Absolutely gorgeous.

Serves 4

Total time: 1 hour 10 minutes

 365 calories

2 cloves garlic

2 onions

2 bulbs fennel

olive oil

1 vegetable bouillon cube

1 x 14-oz can of cannellini beans

1 large egg

2 oz Cheddar cheese

½ teaspoon dried chili flakes

1 teaspoon fennel seeds

3 ½ oz ciabatta or stale bread

4 teaspoons fat-free plain yogurt
   or heavy cream

Peel and finely slice the garlic and onions, then trim and finely slice the fennel (reserving any herby tips for sprinkling at the end). Put all this into a large non-stick saucepan on a medium heat with a lug of oil. Reduce the heat to low, then pop the lid on and cook for around 30 minutes, or until soft and sticky, stirring regularly and adding splashes of water to loosen, if needed. Crumble in the bouillon cube, add the beans (juice and all), then pour in 3 cups of boiling water. Bring to a boil and simmer for 20 minutes. Blitz with an immersion blender to the consistency of your liking, then season to perfection.

Meanwhile, crack the egg into a bowl, grate in the Cheddar and add the chili flakes. Crush the fennel seeds in a pestle and mortar, add to the bowl, then whisk together. Chop the bread into erratic 1 ¼-inch chunks, then toss and scrunch in the egg mixture. Fry in a large non-stick frying pan over a medium heat with a little oil, turning until golden all over.

Divide the soup between your bowls and drizzle with yogurt or cream. Scatter over any reserved fennel tips and add an extra little pinch of chili flakes, if you like, then serve with the tasty French toast croutons.

Roasted squash
– 4 exciting ways

Whole-roasted butternut squash is great to have in the fridge for easy meals and is a brilliant way to utilize spare oven space. Simply roast a whole squash (roughly 2 ½ lbs) at 350°F for 1 hour 30 minutes, then seed, scoop out the flesh, and either use right away or save for another day. One squash makes two of the dishes below.

Squash fritters

Serves 6

Total time: 30 minutes (plus squash roasting time)

Mash half a cooled squash with a heaping ¾ cup of self-rising flour, 1 large egg, 5 oz of cottage cheese and a pinch of pepper. Place a large non-stick frying pan on a medium heat with a lug of olive oil and add heaping tablespoons of the mixture in batches (it should make around 18). Flip when they're golden on the bottom, then add 1 knob of unsalted butter to the center of the pan, pick in a few fresh sage leaves and keep them moving to crisp up. Flip the fritters again to coat them in the infused oil, then cook until beautifully golden on both sides. Nice served with a little grated cheese or a cheeky fried egg on the side.

Squash rigatoni

Serves 4

Total time: 20 minutes (plus squash roasting time)

Put a lug of olive oil and 1 good pinch of dried chili flakes into a large saucepan on a medium heat, then strip in the leaves from 8 sprigs of fresh thyme and squash in 2 cloves of garlic through a garlic press. Fry for 1 minute, then mash in half a squash and stir in 2 tablespoons of reduced-fat crème fraîche, 1 ½ oz of blue cheese and a good splash of boiling water. Simmer gently while you cook 11 oz of dried rigatoni according to package instructions, then drain, reserving a cupful of cooking water. Season the squash mixture to perfection, then toss the pasta through it, loosening with cooking water, if needed. Serve right away with a grating of Parmesan cheese to finish it off.

Squash hummus

Serves 6 to 8

Total time: 15 minutes (plus squash roasting time)

Toast 1 heaping tablespoon of raw sesame seeds in a hot, dry saucepan until golden. On a large board, peel 1 clove of garlic, then finely slice with 1 fresh red chile (seed if you like) and ½ a bunch of fresh cilantro (½ oz), stalks and all. Add half a squash and tip over the toasted seeds. Pour 1 x 14-oz can of chickpeas (juice and all) into the empty pan and bring to a boil, then drain and add to the board with the squash and start chopping, squashing and mixing it all together with the juice of ½ a lemon and an equal amount of extra virgin olive oil until it's the consistency you like. Taste, season to perfection and serve with warm soft flour tortillas.

Squash bruschetta

Serves 2 to 4

Total time: 15 minutes (plus squash roasting time)

Finely slice 2 rashers of smoked bacon and quarter 3 ½ oz of button mushrooms, then fry in a pan on a medium heat with a little olive oil, stirring occasionally. When lightly golden, toss in a few fresh sage leaves and continue frying until golden and crisp. Meanwhile, grill or toast 4 nice slices of bread, then rub them with the cut side of 1 clove of garlic and drizzle with a little extra virgin olive oil. Mash half a squash and season to perfection with salt, pepper and a little grating of Cheddar cheese. Divide the squash and spread rustically across the toasts, then sprinkle over the crispy bacon, mushrooms and sage and serve. Nice with an extra little shaving of Cheddar, if you like.

Baked onion in the hole

Toad in the hole is obviously a great British institution, but I don't want all the veggies out there to miss out, so this is a super-cute version using whole sweet red onions instead of sausages. It could just as easily use portobello mushrooms or chunks of butternut squash, so get creative. With rich onion gravy on the side, it's happy days!

Serves 4
Total time: 1 hour 35 minutes

 273 calories

5 red onions

olive oil

¾ cup all-purpose flour

2 large eggs

⅓ cup reduced-fat milk

½ bunch of fresh thyme (½ oz)

4 fresh bay leaves

optional: 2 tablespoons balsamic vinegar

1 teaspoon English mustard

Worcestershire sauce

1 vegetable bouillon cube

To take this recipe to another level, I like to poke a nugget of blue cheese into the top of each onion as soon as they come out of the oven – it's heavenly.

Preheat the oven to 350°F. Peel 4 of the onions, keeping them whole, then trim the roots so that they'll sit flat. Cut a cross into the top of each, going about three-quarters of the way down and leaving them intact at the root. Season the insides with salt and pepper, then place in a roasting pan (roughly 10 x 12 inches) or divide between four small individual dishes (roughly 6 inches in diameter each – place the dishes in your largest roasting pan to make them easier to handle). Drizzle the onions with oil, cover with aluminum foil and roast for around 1 hour, or until soft.

Meanwhile, put ⅔ cup of flour into a pitcher with a pinch of salt, whisk in the eggs, then gradually add the milk until you have a smooth batter. Pick the thyme leaves. Once the onions are soft, turn the oven up to 425°F. Add a drizzle of oil to the pan or dishes, then put back into the oven to heat up. Once hot, quickly but carefully pour the batter around the onions, then sprinkle over the thyme and bay leaves. Return to the oven and cook for around 30 minutes if making one pan and around 20 minutes if making individual portions, or until puffed up and golden (don't be tempted to open the oven during this time).

Meanwhile, to make the gravy, peel and finely slice the remaining onion, put it into a medium saucepan on a medium heat with a lug of oil and cook for around 15 minutes, or until soft, stirring occasionally. Add the balsamic towards the end (if using) and a splash of water to stop it sticking, if needed. Stir in 1 heaping tablespoon of flour, the mustard and a few swigs of Worcestershire sauce, crumble in the bouillon cube and add 2 ½ cups of boiling water. Simmer for 10 minutes, or until you've got the consistency you're looking for. Remove the pan or dishes from the oven, and serve straight away with the gravy and some seasonal greens on the side.

Really tasty charred Asian salad

This recipe is absolutely delicious. I love transforming veg that you'd usually boil or roast by thinly slicing them and charring them on a grill pan to give the most wonderful, intense, nutty flavor like this – they're incredible dressed with Asian flavors and served with tofu. This recipe is definitely one not to be missed.

Serves 4 to 6
Total time: 1 hour 30 minutes

490 calories

3 carrots

½ butternut squash

1 bunch of scallions

1 head of Napa cabbage

1 head of broccoli

3 ½ oz button mushrooms

5 oz brown rice

1 large thumb-sized piece of gingerroot

1 large clove garlic

1–2 fresh red chiles

1 ½ tablespoons Asian sesame oil

3 tablespoons olive oil

4 tablespoons reduced-sodium soy sauce

1 lemon

12 oz firm tofu

2 tablespoons raw sesame seeds

Get your grill pan on a high heat (use two, if you have them). Start cutting the veg into pieces that are a pleasure to eat, placing them on the dry grill in batches as you go – peel the carrots, seed the squash and slice ¼ inch thick, trim the scallions, break the cabbage leaves apart (halving any really big ones), cut the broccoli into florets and halve the mushrooms or leave whole, depending on their size. The cabbage will only need around 1 minute, the scallions, broccoli and mushrooms 2 to 3 minutes, and the carrots and squash up to 5 minutes. Move the veg to a large platter as and when they're done, cutting the scallions in half after cooking.

Meanwhile, cook the rice according to package instructions. Peel the ginger and garlic, then finely grate them with the chile into a clean jam jar. Add the sesame and olive oils, soy sauce and the juice from the lemon, then pop the lid on and shake to combine. Slice the tofu ½ inch thick, brush all over with some of the dressing and grill until bar-marked on both sides – the tofu will stick to begin with, but as it starts to darken and char, you will be able to peel it away from the grill fairly easily.

When the rice is done, drain it well. Toss the grilled veg, tofu and rice together in the remaining dressing, taste and season to perfection, if needed. Place on a large platter, scatter over the sesame seeds and serve.

Giant veg rösti
Poached eggs, spinach & peas

This is a particularly good breakfast, brunch or lunch. I suppose it's not technically a traditional square meal as we often see it, but it's fulfilling, a lovely contrast of textures and flavors, and a total pleasure to eat. Roasting the spuds and carrots to create the giant rösti really brings out their sweetness, and builds up a nice crunchy edge.

Serves 4

Total time: 55 minutes

351 calories

1 ¼ lbs potatoes

3 large carrots

½ teaspoon Dijon mustard

½ lemon

extra virgin olive oil

olive oil

¾ cup frozen peas

2 cups baby spinach

4 large eggs

2 oz feta cheese

Preheat the oven to 350°F. Peel the potatoes and carrots, then coarsely grate them in a food processor or by hand on a box grater. Add a good pinch of salt, toss and scrunch it all together, then leave for 5 minutes. Meanwhile, mix the mustard, a good squeeze of lemon juice, and a couple of lugs of extra virgin olive oil with a little pinch of salt and pepper in a medium bowl and put aside.

Drizzle a really good lug of olive oil into a large bowl and add a good pinch of pepper. Handful by handful, squeeze the potato and carrot mixture to get rid of the excess salty liquid, then sprinkle into the bowl. Toss in the oil and pepper until well mixed, then evenly scatter it in a large oiled roasting pan (roughly 12 x 16 inches). Roast for around 35 minutes, or until golden on top and super crispy around the edges.

Meanwhile, blanch the peas for a minute in a large saucepan of boiling salted water, then scoop out, add to the bowl of dressing and pile the spinach on top. Just before your rösti is ready, with the water gently simmering, crack in the eggs, poach to your liking, then carefully remove with a slotted spoon. Serve the rösti with the eggs on top. Quickly toss the salad together to dress it and scatter in piles on the rösti, then crumble over the feta and serve. I like to whack it in the middle of the table and let everyone dig in.

Zombie brain

(Magnificent whole-roasted celery root, mushroom sauce & barley)

Mind-blowing flavors come from the slow-roasting of this whole celery root. I'm fully aware that the general scenario and name might seem very weird, but vegetarian, meat-atarian, whoever you are, please open your mind and have a go at this bad boy – it's delicious, fulfilling, funny, and you'll get people talking.

Serves 6

Total time: 2 hours 15 minutes

333 calories

1 large celery root (roughly 2 ½ lbs)

olive oil

6 sprigs of fresh thyme

7 fresh bay leaves

6 cloves garlic

2 tablespoons unsalted butter

1 cup pearl barley

1 small onion

1 ¾ lbs mushrooms

¼ vegetable bouillon cube

⅔ cup heavy cream

1 heaping teaspoon English mustard

extra virgin olive oil

Preheat the oven to 375°F. Scrub the celery root clean, using a brush to clean away any soil from the root. Tear off a double layer of wide aluminum foil and place the celery root in the middle, root-side up. Rub with olive oil, salt and pepper, sprinkle over the thyme sprigs and 6 bay leaves, then bash 4 whole cloves of garlic and scatter over. Pull the sides of the foil up really tightly around the celery root and scrunch around its shape, leaving it open at the top. Place the butter on top of the celery root so that it melts down and around it as it cooks, then fold the foil over really tightly to seal. Place in an ovenproof dish and roast for around 2 hours, or until tender.

Meanwhile, cook the pearl barley at the appropriate time according to package instructions. Peel and finely slice the onion and remaining garlic, place in a large frying pan on a low heat with a lug of olive oil, and fry for around 10 minutes, or until softened, stirring occasionally. Finely slice the mushrooms and add (your pan will be very full, but trust me, they will cook down nicely). Cook for around 20 minutes, or until golden, continuing to stir occasionally. Crumble in the bouillon cube, add the remaining bay leaf and pour in ¾ cup of boiling water. Simmer and reduce until the liquid has nearly evaporated, then stir in the cream and mustard and simmer for a further 5 minutes. Season to perfection and keep warm until needed, being careful not to let it get too thick.

Around 10 minutes before the celery root is ready, carefully open up the foil and start basting every couple of minutes with the melted butter for extra color. Drain the pearl barley and dress it with salt, pepper and extra virgin olive oil. Place the celery root on a board and carve thinly, like you would a joint of meat. Drizzle with any juices from the foil, then serve with the mushroom sauce, pearl barley and lots of beautiful seasonal greens.

Contrary to perception, truffle oil in little bottles can be picked up in most supermarkets fairly cheaply, and half a teaspoon will very subtly transform this sauce to make it even more delicious, so add some if you've got it.

Sweet potato & spinach frittata

It's always good to have some nice egg recipes up your sleeve – they're a great-value protein, delicious, and a frittata still gives me the same feeling of happiness I'd get from a quiche, pie or pizza. Best served hot, although, frankly, it's lovely cold or at room temperature, in a packed lunch or as part of a picnic with salad and cured meats too.

Serves 4 to 6
Total time: 1 hour 15 minutes

423 calories

2 medium sweet potatoes

olive oil

10 oz frozen spinach

1 whole nutmeg, for grating

8 large eggs

2 ½ oz feta cheese

1 ½ oz Cheddar cheese

Preheat the oven to 375°F. Scrub the sweet potatoes clean, then rub them with a little salt, pepper and oil and place on a baking sheet. Roast for about 50 minutes, or until soft and cooked through, then leave aside until they're cool enough to handle.

Place an 11-inch non-stick ovenproof frying pan on a medium heat, put in a lug of oil, the spinach, a pinch of salt and pepper and a good grating of nutmeg, and cook until the spinach is wilted, stirring occasionally until all the liquid has evaporated. Meanwhile, crack the eggs into a mixing bowl, season lightly, whisk up, then crumble in half the feta and grate in half the Cheddar.

Remove the pan from the heat – you should try to do this next part quite quickly: pour in the egg mixture and give it a really good stir. Rip in bombs of sweet potato (you can discard the skins if you want to, but I rather like the nutty flavor), then break over the remaining feta and grate over the rest of the Cheddar. Bang the pan straight into the oven for 13 to 15 minutes, or until fluffy and golden. Serve straight from the pan or turn out onto a board. Lovely served with a simple lemony-dressed green salad.

This recipe uses frozen spinach to great effect, so it can be made all year round, but the point of a frittata is that it can embrace most veg when in season, at their best and generally their cheapest – peas, asparagus, crumbled baby potatoes, broccoli, the list goes on . . .

Eggplant daal
Handmade chapattis

If you cook this daal well and season it with love, it'll be delicious, incredibly economical and sociable, fun eating. Our tasty friend Mr Daal does have the tendency to be quite ugly, but I think – rolled up in these handmade chapattis with fluffy rice, roasted eggplant, crispy curry leaves and chile, then presented to one's gob – it's a beautiful experience. So I say no more ugly daal, dress it up, baby, because it's all about the confidence!

Serves 6

Total time: 1 hour 50 minutes

525 calories

1 large eggplant

2 red onions

4 cloves garlic

2 thumb-sized pieces of gingerroot

4 tablespoons rogan josh curry paste

peanut oil

1 lb yellow split peas

1 vegetable bouillon cube

1 ½ cups wholewheat flour, plus extra
   for dusting

2 tablespoons olive oil

1 mug (10 oz) of basmati rice

1 fresh red chile

1 handful of fresh or dried curry leaves

1 teaspoon mustard seeds

Preheat the oven to 350°F. Cut the eggplant into ¾-inch chunks, peel and slice the onions and garlic, then peel and finely grate the ginger. Put all this into a large high-sided roasting pan with the curry paste and a lug of peanut oil. Toss together until well coated, then roast for 20 to 25 minutes, or until sticky and caramelized. Remove half the roasted veg to a large saucepan to start your daal and return the pan to the oven to keep warm – turn the oven off so that the veg don't dry out. Place the saucepan on a low heat on the stove. Stir in the split peas, crumble in the bouillon cube and add 8 cups of boiling water. Simmer for around 1 hour 20 minutes with the lid on, or until the split peas are tender and the daal has thickened, stirring occasionally, and adding splashes of water to loosen, if needed.

Meanwhile, place the flour in a large bowl with a pinch of salt and make a well in the middle. Add the olive oil and ⅔ cup of water to the well and mix together with a fork. When it comes together as dough, tip it onto a flour-dusted surface, knead until smooth, then divide into 12 balls. Roll each one into a circle, nice and thin, turning as you go and dusting with a little extra flour, if needed. Put a frying pan on a medium heat and cook the chapattis for 1 minute on each side, or until cooked but not colored. Stack them in aluminum foil as you go and keep them warm until needed.

Put 1 mug of rice and 2 mugs of boiling water into a saucepan with a pinch of salt. Cook on a medium heat with the lid on for 12 minutes, or until all the liquid has been absorbed. Meanwhile, to make the flavored oil (called a temper), finely slice the chile and place it in a small frying pan on a medium heat with the curry leaves, mustard seeds and a good lug of peanut oil for 1 to 2 minutes, or until crispy. Load up your warm chapattis with rice, daal and a scattering of roasted veggies, drizzle over the temper, roll up and tuck in.

Pappa alle zucchine
(Zucchini & bread soup)

This amazing beauty of a soup is based on the Italian classic pappa al pomodoro (tomato and bread soup). It's a principle you can embrace with lots of different veg, as it's essentially about cooking them low and slow to bring out their deep flavor and sweetness, then pairing them with some bread to add a bit of body. I've used zucchini here, which are great when they're in season, but it would also work well with fennel, peas, leeks or asparagus.

Serves 4
Total time: 1 hour 35 minutes

209 calories

2 onions

2 cloves garlic

4 zucchini

olive oil

1 vegetable bouillon cube

½ loaf of ciabatta or stale bread

extra virgin olive oil

½ bunch of fresh mint (½ oz)

Peel and finely slice the onions and garlic, then trim the zucchini and halve lengthways, cut away the fluffy core and finely slice them. Put all these into a large saucepan on a medium-low heat with a lug of olive oil. Cook slowly for around 1 hour 15 minutes, stirring occasionally and adding a splash of water, if needed – you want the zucchini and onions to really cook down, and get super soft and caramelized – go gently, and in return you get big flavor.

Once the time's up, crumble in the bouillon cube and tear in the bread in quite rough chunks. Pour in 4 cups of boiling water, bring back to a boil, then simmer for a further 10 minutes, or until thick and delicious. Season to perfection, add a good drizzle of extra virgin olive oil, then finely chop the mint leaves and stir into the soup. Divide between your bowls and tuck in.

Just like the sausage panzanella (see page 180), this recipe is perfect for using up stale bread, helping you waste less.

If you bought small or medium zucchini, or you've grown your own, they won't be fluffy in the middle, so you won't need to cut out the core. And, if you've grown your own, you'll also get the wonderful zucchini flowers for free, which will live very happily torn into the soup right at the end, adding an extra splash of color.

The best cauliflower & broccoli cheese

Cauliflower cheese has always been a big favorite in the Oliver household. I have to be honest, it's such a staple I never thought I could do it better, but this version really has the edge, with broccoli mushed into the white sauce and the beautiful crunch of almonds and bread crumbs on top – it's epic! Good-value frozen broccoli and cauliflower are perfect for this kind of cooking, and remember, the better the cheese, the better the dish.

Serves 8 as a side

Total time: 1 hour 35 minutes

267 calories

2 cloves garlic

3 ½ tablespoons unsalted butter

⅓ cup all-purpose flour

2 cups reduced-fat (2%) milk

1 lb fresh or frozen broccoli

2 ½ oz sharp Cheddar cheese

2 lbs fresh or frozen cauliflower

2 slices of ciabatta or stale bread

2 sprigs of fresh thyme

1 oz sliced almonds

olive oil

Preheat the oven to 350°F. Peel and finely slice the garlic and put it into a medium saucepan on a medium heat with the butter. When the butter has melted, stir in the flour for a minute to make a paste, then gradually add the milk, whisking as you go, until lovely and smooth. Add the broccoli (cut up first, if using fresh) and simmer for around 20 minutes, or until the broccoli is cooked through and starts to break down, then mash or blitz with an immersion blender (adding an extra splash of milk to loosen, if using fresh broccoli). Grate in half the Cheddar and season to perfection.

Arrange the cauliflower in an appropriately sized baking dish (cut into florets first, if using fresh), pour over the broccoli white sauce and grate over the remaining Cheddar. Blitz the bread into bread crumbs in a food processor, then pulse in the thyme leaves and almonds. Toss with a lug of oil and a pinch of salt and pepper, then scatter evenly over the cauliflower cheese. Bake for 1 hour, or until golden and cooked through, then enjoy!

It's really good fun to play around with different cheeses in this dish and how they taste and melt. It's also nice to try different veg instead of cauliflower – for instance, ¾–1 ¼-inch chunks of celery root, squash, potatoes or leeks would all work a treat. Have a play and see what your favorites are – some veg might take longer to cook than others, so test with a knife to check they're cooked through before serving.

BBQ baked beans
Smashed sweet potatoes

Comforting and delicious, this is great served as a meat-free dinner or, without the killer croutons, it makes a damn fine side dish at any barbecue or with roasted meats. Feel free to use canned butter beans or even chickpeas in this recipe if they're your favorites — this is the ultimate in baked beans, so make it your own.

Serves 6

Total time: 1 hour 25 minutes

2 red onions

2 cloves garlic

1 fresh red chile

2 large carrots

olive oil

1 heaping teaspoon sweet smoked paprika

1 level teaspoon cumin seeds

1 level teaspoon dried chili flakes

6 medium sweet potatoes

3 ¼ cups passata

2 x 14-oz cans of mixed beans

⅓ cup BBQ sauce

a few sprigs of fresh rosemary

½ loaf of ciabatta or stale bread

optional: 1 ½ oz Cheddar cheese

fat-free plain yogurt, to serve

Preheat the oven to 350°F. Peel the onions and garlic, then finely slice with the chile. Peel and chop the carrots. Put all these into a large roasting pan and place on a medium heat with a lug of oil, the paprika, cumin seeds and chili flakes. Cook for 20 minutes, or until softened, stirring regularly. Meanwhile, scrub the sweet potatoes clean, then rub them with a little oil, salt and pepper, place on a baking sheet and put aside.

When the time's up, stir the passata into the pan, add a splash of water to the empty jar, swirl it around and pour it in along with the beans (juice and all). Drizzle over the BBQ sauce, season lightly with salt and pepper and stir well. Pick and roughly chop the rosemary leaves, toss in a little oil and sprinkle over the top, then place in the oven for around 1 hour, or until bubbling, baked and gorgeous, adding a splash or two of water to loosen, if needed. Put the baking sheet of sweet potatoes into the oven for the same amount of time, or until soft and cooked through.

Around 20 minutes before the beans are ready, tear the bread into rough chunks and toss with a drizzle of oil in a roasting pan. Grate over the Cheddar (if using), then place on the bottom shelf of the oven for around 15 minutes, or until crispy and golden, to make croutons.

Remove everything from the oven, tear up or squidge open the potatoes, and serve with the beans, dollops of yogurt and the homemade croutons to mop up that delicious sauce, with a simple green salad on the side.

Beet fritters
Dressed lentils & leaves

This was one of the last recipes I wrote for this book – I wanted to add an extra, really exciting salad that bigs up the humble beet and treats famously boring lentils right so that they're delicious and really sing. Me and my testing team absolutely love this dish – it's beautiful, tasty and nutritious. I hope you love it too.

Serves 4
Total time: 40 minutes

426 calories

8 oz Puy lentils

1 red onion

3 tablespoons red wine vinegar

3 tablespoons extra virgin olive oil

1 teaspoon English mustard

1 14-oz can whole small beets

1 heaping teaspoon grated horseradish
   (from a jar)

1 large egg

2 tablespoons all-purpose flour

7 oz cottage cheese

olive oil

1 head of bibb lettuce

Cook the lentils according to package instructions, then drain, reserving a little cooking water. Meanwhile, peel the onion, then, on a mandolin (use the guard!) or with good knife skills, very finely slice it. Place it in a bowl, add 1 tablespoon of vinegar and a good pinch of salt, then scrunch and toss together to make a quick pickle, and put aside.

In a separate bowl, mix the extra virgin olive oil, the remaining vinegar and the mustard with 1 tablespoon of juice from the beet can. Season to perfection, then put a little of the dressing aside for drizzling later. Toss the rest of the dressing with the lentils, loosening with a splash of reserved cooking water, if needed.

Mix the horseradish, egg and flour together in a bowl, then fold in the cottage cheese and season well. Drain the beets and chop a similar size to the cottage cheese curds (you might want to wear rubber gloves to do this), then fold through the mixture to create a rippled effect. Place a large non-stick frying pan on a medium heat and add a lug of olive oil. Fry heaping teaspoons of the beet mixture for 2 to 3 minutes on each side, or until golden. Meanwhile, trim the stalk off the lettuce and break the leaves apart.

Squeeze the onion to get rid of the excess salty liquid, then you're ready to portion up. Start with lentils, followed by the lettuce leaves, quick pickle and fritters, then drizzle with the remaining dressing. Delicious.

Happy frumpy minestrone

When the fridge is bare, it's very easy to make this hearty minestrone from staples you've got in your cupboards and freezer, including all those little annoying pasta ends you've got lying around, left in packages and cluttering up your shelves. This frumpy soup is super tasty – it might not be a good looker, but it goes down a treat. Happiness.

Serves 6
Total time: 1 hour

449 calories

2 onions

2 lbs mixture of carrots, celery root
  and butternut squash

olive oil

1 vegetable bouillon cube

1 x 14-oz can of diced tomatoes

1 x 14-oz can of romano beans

7 oz mixed dried pasta

7 oz frozen spinach

7 oz mixture of frozen peas
  and fava beans

½ loaf of ciabatta or stale bread

1 oz Parmesan cheese

optional: red wine

extra virgin olive oil

Preheat the oven to 350°F. Peel the onions, carrots, celery root and squash, cut into ½-inch dice and put into a large pan with a good lug of olive oil. Cook for around 10 minutes on a medium heat, stirring occasionally, then crumble in the bouillon cube and add the tomatoes, the beans and their juice and 8 cups of boiling water. Bring to a boil, then reduce to a simmer for 30 minutes. Smash up and chuck in the pasta, along with the spinach, peas and fava beans, for the last 10 minutes.

Meanwhile, tear the bread into rough chunks and toss in a roasting pan with pepper and olive oil. Finely grate over most of the Parmesan, then roast for 20 to 25 minutes, or until golden and crispy, turning halfway.

Season the soup to perfection, adding a swig of red wine (if you have it), then drizzle with a little extra virgin olive oil and grate over the remaining Parmesan. Serve with the crunchy rustic croutons on the side.

You can use pretty much any combo of fresh and frozen veggies for this dish – throw in whatever you've got on hand. A few fresh herbs work beautifully too, so chop and add these if you've got them.

HAVE YOU EVER ...
OPENED A BOTTLE OF WINE & NOT QUITE FINISHED IT?

If not, you might need to go to AA. . . . but seriously, many people don't polish off every bottle of wine they open and often waste that last bit. If this is you, don't throw it away – have a go at making your own delicious vinegar. If you read up or get online, you'll find lots of in-depth methods, but this is how I like to do it. It's fun and brings out your inner geek, and the finished product is generally better than what you'd buy because it has half-decent wine going into it. Without doubt, vinegar is one of the most important and underrated pantry ingredients. It has the ability to totally transform your cooking, so use it with confidence and authority. That contrast of rich and fatty flavors with vinegar and pickles is amazing. That's why having pickles in a kebab, and vinegary mint sauce with lamb, is so good. Vinegar is also a wonderful stomach settler, and helps you digest rich foods. Give it a go.

There are two main, easy ways you can have a go at making your own vinegar. To start off with, you need a bacteria called a vinegar "mother" to essentially spoil wine and turn it into acidic vinegar. These spores are floating around in the atmosphere invisibly all the time. So, to start off your vinegar-making, leave a couple of half-empty bottles of any vinegar with the lids off in a dark cupboard at 60 to 80°F. After a couple of weeks the vinegar will go a bit cloudy, there'll be some sediment at the bottom and there'll be a kinda skin floating around. It sounds gross, but this is good news – it's the "mother." One important thing to remember is that you must never touch the "mother" with metal, as the resulting chemical reaction will kill the culture, so be careful!

Now you've got two choices – you can either start adding your wine dregs to these vinegar bottles, or you can decant them into a large earthenware jar with a plate as a lid, or a vinegar crock with a cork and a tap (buy online or from junk shops). Simply add the vinegar "mother" and the dregs of your wine, and to be honest, after a couple of weeks, I use the vinegar whenever I want, topping it up whenever I've got any wine dregs. Every time you're cooking, give it a shake to put oxygen through the vinegar. If you want to keep it to just white or red wine vinegar, keep them separate in that way, but personally I just have one house vinegar, which works a treat.

The second way to make the wine "mother," which is simple and fun, is to mix your wine dregs together until you've just over half-filled a wine bottle, pop the cork in, and wrap it in plastic wrap and a kitchen towel. Keep it in the trunk of your car and let it roll around for a month of regular driving – this seems to agitate it well and encourages it to form its own "mother."

Making flavored vinegars to use in cooking is also a great thing to do. They're dead easy, will add incredible flavor to dressings, are brilliant drizzled over meats or added to stews or chilis, and of course vinegars work really well for preserving, pickling and chutneys. Simply decant your vinegar into a nice bottle, add your chosen flavorings, then seal, label and pop on the shelf. Mixed fresh herbs, berries, chiles, toasted spices like cinnamon, allspice and mustard seeds with peppercorns and strips of citrus zest all work a treat.

Simple tomato pasta
– 4 fantastic ways

Here are four ways me and my family enjoy a good old tomato pasta. So simple, so quick and so tasty – enjoy.

Arrabbiata
Serves 4

374 calories

Total time: 20 minutes

Halve 1 fresh red chile lengthways and put into a large saucepan on a medium heat with a lug of olive oil while you peel and finely slice 2 cloves of garlic. Add to the pan with 1 pinch of dried chili flakes and fry for 1 minute, then pour in 2 x 14-oz cans of diced tomatoes. Add a splash of water to one of the empty cans, swirl it around and add to the pan. Bring to a boil, then reduce to a gentle simmer for around 15 minutes. Meanwhile, cook 11 oz of dried spaghetti according to package instructions and drain, reserving a cupful of cooking water. Season the sauce to perfection, then toss the pasta through it, loosening with cooking water, if needed. Serve sprinkled with a few fresh baby basil leaves.

Caponata
Serves 4

367 calories

Total time: 35 minutes

Cut 1 large eggplant into ½-inch cubes and fry in a large saucepan on a medium heat with a lug of olive oil for 15 minutes, stirring often. Add 1 tablespoon each of brown sugar and red wine vinegar. Peel and finely slice 2 cloves of garlic, add to the pan and fry for 1 minute. Pour in 2 x 14-oz cans of diced tomatoes, add a splash of water to one of the empty cans, swirl it around and add to the pan. Bring to a boil, then reduce to a gentle simmer for around 15 minutes. Meanwhile, cook 11 oz of dried tagliatelle according to package instructions and drain, reserving a cupful of cooking water. Season the sauce to perfection, then toss the pasta through it, loosening with cooking water, if needed. Serve with a grating of Parmesan cheese.

Peperonata
Serves 4

369 calories

Total time: 35 minutes

Seed and finely dice 2 bell peppers and cook in a large saucepan on a medium-low heat with a lug of olive oil for 15 minutes, stirring regularly. Peel and finely slice 2 cloves of garlic, add to the pan and fry for 1 minute, then add 1 tablespoon of red wine vinegar and 2 x 14-oz cans of diced tomatoes. Add a splash of water to one of the empty cans, swirl it around and add to the pan. Bring to a boil, then reduce to a gentle simmer for around 15 minutes. Meanwhile, cook 11 oz of dried penne according to package instructions and drain, reserving a cupful of cooking water. Season the sauce to perfection, then toss the pasta through it, loosening with cooking water, if needed. Serve with a grating of Parmesan cheese.

Puttanesca
Serves 4

430 calories

Total time: 20 minutes

Bash 16 black olives and remove the pits, peel and finely slice 2 cloves of garlic, and put both of these into a large saucepan on a medium heat with a lug of olive oil, 1 heaping teaspoon of capers and 1 pinch of dried chili flakes. Fry for a couple of minutes, then pour in 2 x 14-oz cans of diced tomatoes. Add a splash of water to one of the empty cans, swirl it around and add to the pan. Drain and flake in 1 x 6-oz can of tuna, bring to a boil, then reduce to a gentle simmer for around 15 minutes. Meanwhile, cook 11 oz of dried pasta shells according to package instructions and drain, reserving a cupful of cooking water. Toss the pasta through the sauce, loosening with cooking water, if needed. Serve with a grating of lemon zest for added zing.

Okonomiyaki
(Epic savory Japanese pancake)

Okonomi means "whatever you like," and basically this pancake, like a traditional savory British pancake, exists to use up leftovers or seasonal ingredients. In recent years in Japan, and around the world, this dish has catapulted into pizza territory in terms of its versatility and popularity – everyone loves it. So here's a really good expression that I love, embracing tofu, mushrooms, radishes and cabbage. It's a pleasure to eat.

Serves 6

Total time: 30 minutes

269 calories

1 onion

3 ½ oz button mushrooms

½ head of Napa or Savoy cabbage

3 ½ oz radishes

12 oz silken tofu

6 large eggs

1 cup all-purpose flour

olive oil

tomato ketchup or hot chili sauce

reduced-sodium soy sauce

mayo or fat-free plain yogurt

Peel the onion, then finely slice it with the mushrooms, cabbage (removing any tough stems) and radishes. Pat the tofu dry with paper towel and cut into ½-inch cubes. Whisk the eggs and flour together until smooth, season well, then fold in the tofu and vegetables until well combined.

Put a lug of oil into an 11-inch non-stick frying pan on a medium heat with half the mixture. Cook for 4 to 5 minutes on each side, or until golden and cooked through – if you're feeling confident, go for it and flip it in the pan, but if not, turn it out onto a plate, then carefully slide it back in. Serve the okonomiyaki straight away, drizzled with ketchup or chili sauce, soy sauce and some mayo or yogurt (you can do it straight from the bottle or jar, but I like to put the sauces in sandwich bags, snip off a corner, and squeeze them over the top in cute lines). Repeat with the remaining ingredients.

To make a tasty, quick Japanese pickle to serve on the side, halve ½ an English cucumber lengthways and scrape out the seeds, then finely slice it and roughly scrunch it in a bowl with 1 pinch of dried chili flakes and a lug each of soy sauce, Asian sesame oil and white wine vinegar.

CHICKEN

• CHICKEN RECIPES •

Chicken is the most popular meat that's searched for on the Internet, so to reflect its popularity this is the biggest meat chapter in the book. There's a classic Sunday roast, which is guaranteed to give leftover meat, so more recipes follow, all making use of those leftovers or utilizing the carcass in a delicious way. Then there are lots of tasty dishes that stretch a small amount of chicken a lot further, or show you how versatile the cheaper cuts can be. I go for pasture-raised chicken, but if you want cheaper chicken without compromising on flavor or welfare, please as a minimum choose a bird approved by Certified Humane. These are commercially farmed higher-welfare birds, and I can honestly say I would feed them to my family. Start here, and upgrade to pasture-raised or organic whenever you can.

MOTHERSHIP SUNDAY ROAST CHICKEN

This is my ultimate roast chicken. The secret to juiciness, flavor and quick cooking is putting a whole hot pricked lemon that's been parboiling with the spuds into the cavity, and letting that help the chicken cook from the inside while it roasts on the outside. I've also given you rock-solid recipes for gravy and accompaniments.

Serves 4 plus leftovers

Total time: 2 hours

2 lbs potatoes

1 lemon

4 sprigs of fresh rosemary

1 x 4-lb whole chicken

olive oil

1 lb carrots

1 onion

2 knobs of unsalted butter

1 orange

2 sprigs of fresh thyme

2 cloves garlic

1 heaping tablespoon all-purpose flour

½ head of Savoy cabbage

1 ¾ cups frozen peas

Once cooked, carefully pull the lemon out of the chicken, let it cool, then pop it into the fridge. Finely chop it and add it to any couscous, bulgur or rice dish to add an extra flavor dimension.

Preheat the oven to 400°F. Peel the potatoes, halving any larger ones, then parboil in a large saucepan of boiling salted water with the lemon for 12 minutes. Meanwhile, strip half the rosemary leaves into a pestle and mortar and smash with a good pinch of salt and pepper, then in a roasting pan, rub all over the chicken really well with a lug of oil. Peel the carrots and onion, then cut the onion into 8 wedges and place under the chicken with the carrot peelings. Cut the carrots at an angle into 1 ¼-inch chunks and tip into a snug-fitting roasting pan with 1 knob of butter. Peel in strips of orange zest, then squeeze in the juice. Strip in the thyme leaves, add a pinch of salt and pepper and toss to coat, then cover with aluminum foil and put aside.

Drain the potatoes and shake to fluff up. Use tongs to remove the lemon, prick it with a knife and push it into the cavity of the chicken. Roast the chicken for 1 hour 20 minutes, or until golden and cooked through. Tip the potatoes into a roasting pan with a lug of oil and a pinch of salt and pepper and strip over the remaining rosemary leaves. Smash the garlic and add to the pan, toss well and roast alongside the carrots, under the chicken pan, for its last hour, or until golden, shaking both every now and again.

Remove the chicken from the oven, transfer to a platter and cover (leaving the potatoes and carrots in). Spoon the dripping out of the chicken pan and into a clean jam jar for another day (see page 158). Put the pan on a medium heat on the stove and stir in the flour, then pour in 2 ½ cups of boiling water and any chicken resting juices. Stir well and simmer until you've got the consistency you're looking for, then pour and push the gravy through a sieve into a pitcher. Trim away the core of the cabbage, then separate out the leaves and cook in boiling salted water for 5 minutes, adding the peas for the last couple of minutes. Drain and toss with the remaining butter. Serve everything in the middle of the table, with all your usual trimmings.

SINGAPORE NOODLES

 LEFTOVER...

Singapore noodles is a scrumptiously wonderful classic that makes you feel fulfilled and happy. For me, its spirit is that it can easily embrace lots of different leftovers, and it can become a vegetarian option very simply. So, feel free to let this recipe help you waste less, using up whatever you've got in the fridge.

Serves 4 to 6
Total time: 30 minutes

470 calories

8 oz fine rice noodles

1 tablespoon unsalted blanched peanuts

5 oz ground pork

olive oil

1 heaping teaspoon curry powder

1 level teaspoon Chinese five-spice powder

1 clove garlic

1 thumb-sized piece of gingerroot

5 oz leftover cooked chicken

4 button or cremini mushrooms

½ head of white cabbage

5 oz frozen peeled cooked shrimp

1 ½ cups frozen peas

2 large eggs

reduced-sodium soy sauce

1 lime

1–2 fresh red chiles

4 scallions

Make sure you have all your ingredients lined up and ready to go. Put the noodles into a bowl, cover with boiling water, leave aside to rehydrate for 5 minutes, or until softened, then drain. Crush the peanuts in a pestle and mortar and toast in a large frying pan or wok on a medium heat until golden. Tip out and put aside, returning the pan to the heat. Put the ground pork into the pan with a lug of oil, the curry powder and five-spice. Stir and fry for 5 minutes, or until lightly golden, while you peel and finely chop the garlic and ginger, and slice the chicken, mushrooms and cabbage.

Keeping things moving, stir the garlic, ginger, chicken and shrimp into the pan, followed a minute later by the mushrooms, cabbage and peas. Toss and cook for 4 minutes, then push everything to one side of the pan and crack the eggs into the gap – stir them around so they start to scramble and cook. Tip in the noodles, then toss everything together for a couple of minutes. Taste and season to perfection with soy sauce, then squeeze over the lime juice and tip onto a large platter. Trim, finely slice and sprinkle over the chile and scallions, scatter over the peanuts and eat right away.

FRENCHIE SALAD

LEFTOVER...

I love this Frenchie salad – it really bigs up French beans and makes lentils taste great. Don't be afraid of going heavy on the mustard, because that's what makes the lentils, beans and chicken really sing. This is great for using up any bits of leftover sweet white meat from under the bird or crispy chicken skin – both of which will be superb.

Serves 4

Total time: 45 minutes

478
calories

8 oz Puy lentils

extra virgin olive oil

cider or white wine vinegar

optional: 2 scallions

1 clove garlic

2 ½ teaspoons Dijon mustard

1 teaspoon honey

2 large eggs

7 oz French beans

7 oz leftover cooked chicken

optional: 4 sprigs of fresh tarragon

1 large round head of bibb lettuce

Cook the lentils according to package instructions, then drain, reserving a little cooking water. Return both to the saucepan and mix in a lug each of oil and vinegar. Season to perfection and leave with the lid on to keep warm.

Trim and finely slice the scallions (if using) and put them into a bowl. Squash in the garlic through a garlic press, then stir in the mustard, honey, 1 tablespoon of vinegar, 3 tablespoons of oil and a pinch of salt and pepper. Mix well to make a dressing, and put aside.

Boil the eggs in a saucepan of boiling salted water for 6 minutes, then scoop out with a slotted spoon and run them under cold water to cool. Trim the ends off the beans, then add the beans to the water to blanch for 4 minutes, or until just cooked but not squeaky when you bite into one. Meanwhile, shred the chicken. Drain the beans, and while they're still hot, toss with a little dressing, the chicken and tarragon leaves (if using).

Tip the warm dressed lentils onto a large platter. Shred the outer leaves of the lettuce, cut the center into quarters and arrange on top of the lentils. Sprinkle over the dressed beans and chicken, drizzle over the remaining dressing, and toss it all together. Peel and quarter the eggs and pop them in and around the salad, then tuck in.

 If you've got a little less chicken left over than the amount I've suggested here, I find that adding an extra egg or two, or chucking in some dressed chickpeas or butter beans, will give you a good balance.

HUMBLE CHICKEN STEW — 4 WAYS

A simple delicious chicken stew done my four favorite ways — choose which one to go for and enjoy.

Strip up to 10 oz of meat off 1 leftover chicken carcass, and put aside. Place the carcass and any bones in a large saucepan and bash up the bones. Cover with 4 cups of water, bring to a boil, then simmer for at least 30 minutes, skimming away any scum from the surface. Meanwhile, finely slice 4 rashers of smoked bacon and place in a large casserole pan on a medium heat with a lug of olive oil, while you peel and chop 2 onions, 3 large carrots, and 2 potatoes or 8 oz of celery root into 1-inch dice. Add to the pan along with a few sprigs of fresh thyme and 2 fresh bay leaves. Cook for 10 minutes, stirring regularly. Halve and stir in 7 oz of button mushrooms, along with the leftover chicken and 1 heaping tablespoon of all-purpose flour. Pour the broth through a sieve straight into the pan (topping up with a little water, if needed) and let it simmer for 40 minutes, or until thick and delicious, while you start your chosen topping. Season to perfection and serve with some seasonal greens.

CHICKEN PIE

511 calories

Serves 6

Total time: 2 hours including stew

Pulse ½ cup of cold unsalted butter, 1 ⅔ cups of all-purpose flour and a pinch of salt in a food processor, then add 4 tablespoons of water to bring it together. Wrap in plastic wrap and refrigerate for 30 minutes. Preheat the oven to 375°F. Transfer the stew to a baking dish (roughly 10 x 12 inches) and eggwash the sides. Roll the dough out on a flour-dusted surface, then place on top of the dish. Pinch the edges to seal, score the middle, eggwash and bake for 30 minutes (40 minutes if the stew is cold), or until golden and hot through.

CHICKEN LASAGNE

424 calories

Serves 4

Total time: 2 hours 20 minutes including stew

Preheat the oven to 375°F. Make a white sauce by melting 3 ½ tablespoons of unsalted butter in a pan on a medium heat. Whisk in ⅓ cup of all-purpose flour to make a paste, then gradually add 2 ¾ cups of reduced-fat (2%) milk, whisking constantly. Simmer until fairly thick, season to perfection, then layer up in a baking dish (roughly 10 x 12 inches) with the stew (add a splash of water to loosen) and 8 oz of fresh lasagne sheets. Finish with a layer of sauce and a nice grating of sharp Cheddar cheese, and bake for 40 minutes, or until golden, bubbling and hot through.

CHICKEN STEW & MASH

332 calories

Serves 4

Total time: 1 hour 50 minutes including stew

Wash and peel 1 ¾ lbs of potatoes, cut into even-sized chunks and cook in a saucepan of boiling salted water for about 20 minutes, or until cooked through. Drain and mash well with a large knob of unsalted butter, 4 tablespoons of reduced-fat (2%) milk and a few scrapings of nutmeg (if you have it). Season to perfection and serve with your hot stew, or you could transfer the stew to a baking dish (roughly 10 x 12 inches), top it with the mash and bake at 375°F for around 20 minutes, or until golden and hot through.

CHICKEN STEW & DUMPLINGS

493 calories

Serves 4

Total time: 1 hour 40 minutes including stew

Place 2 cups of self-rising flour in a mixing bowl. Coarsely grate in ½ cup of cold unsalted butter and rub together until it resembles bread crumbs. Add ⅓ cup of cold water and bring into a ball of dough. Divide into 12 pieces and roll into balls. Loosen the stew with a good splash of water if needed and, when the stew has had 20 of the final 40 minutes, transfer it to an ovenproof pan and place the balls on top. Pop the lid on and bake at 375°F for 30 minutes, or until hot through and the dumplings are fluffy and cooked.

ROAST CHICKEN & SWEET PEA RISOTTO

LEFTOVER…

A well-made risotto is often seen as exciting restaurant food these days, but this fantastic northern Italian short, stubby, starchy rice makes the most silky, elegant dishes and has always been embraced by thrifty Italians. It's perfect for making meals on a budget, and with leftover chicken and sweet peas, this is one of my favorites.

Serves 4

Total time: 1 hour 20 minutes

475 calories

1 leftover chicken carcass,
   plus any leftover cooked chicken

2 onions

olive oil

10 oz risotto or Arborio rice

1 ½ cups frozen peas

1 knob of unsalted butter

2 oz Parmesan cheese

extra virgin olive oil

optional: 2 large handfuls of arugula

To make your broth, strip all the meat you can find off the chicken carcass, shred and put to one side. Place the carcass and any bones in a large saucepan and bash up the bones. Cover with 8 cups of water, bring to a boil, and simmer for at least 30 minutes, skimming away any scum from the surface. Keep warm on the lowest heat, and sieve before using.

Meanwhile, peel and finely chop the onions and put them into a large saucepan on a low heat with a lug of olive oil. Cook for around 15 minutes, or until softened but not colored, stirring occasionally. Stir in the rice for a couple of minutes, then turn the heat up to high and add a ladleful of broth. Let it sizzle and reduce for a few minutes, then, once it's evaporated, add the remaining broth a ladleful at a time, only adding more once each ladleful has been absorbed, and stirring regularly for 16 minutes in total. Add the frozen peas and any leftover chicken if you have it, and cook for a few more minutes or until the rice is cooked but still holds its shape, adding a final splash of broth or water to give you a loose, oozy consistency.

Now's the time to beat in the butter, grate in most of the Parmesan and season the risotto to perfection. Remove from the heat, cover with a lid and leave to sit for 2 minutes, then stir well. Finish with a drizzle of extra virgin olive oil, grate over the remaining Parmesan and serve with a good sprinkling of arugula (if using) on each portion.

If you have a bottle of white wine on the go, add ⅓ cup before you start adding the broth and cook it away before carrying on with the recipe. This will add a wonderful perfume to your risotto.

Often it can be cheaper to use good-quality Cheddar cheese rather than Parmesan and, although not authentic, it makes a brilliant risotto, so you can save a few pennies there too, if you want to.

SMOKIN' CHICKEN CHOWDER

LEFTOVER...

Every time I eat this soup it makes me incredibly happy. The leftover chicken and the broth made from its carcass give a real depth and heartiness, and the hits of corn and crunchy smoky bacon bring it together to make it an absolute pleasure to eat. It's a nice sociable dish to make for friends, served from a pan in the middle of the table.

Serves 6
Total time: 45 minutes

292 calories

1 leftover chicken carcass, plus up to 7 oz leftover cooked chicken

1 onion

2 carrots

1 large potato

optional: ½ bunch of fresh Italian parsley (½ oz)

4 rashers of smoked bacon

2 cups frozen corn

⅓ cup heavy cream

1 handful of cream or matzo crackers

Of course, there are many variations on a chowder, and if you've got a handful of clams you can throw them in – it's only going to make the party better.

Start by getting the broth on the go. Strip all the meat you can find off the chicken carcass, shred and put to one side. Place the carcass and any bones in a large saucepan and bash up the bones. Cover with 8 cups of water, bring to a boil, then simmer for at least 30 minutes, skimming away any scum from the surface.

Meanwhile, peel the onion, carrots and potato and cut into ½-inch dice. Finely slice the parsley stalks (if using) and the bacon. Fry the bacon in a large saucepan on a medium heat until golden and crispy, then remove with a slotted spoon and put aside, leaving the pan on the heat. Add the onion, carrots, potato and parsley stalks (if using) to the pan of tasty bacon fat and cook for around 25 minutes, or until soft, stirring regularly.

Pour the broth through a sieve into the veg pan. Add the corn and leftover chicken, then bring to a boil and simmer for 5 minutes. Use an immersion blender to whiz up about a quarter of the soup until smooth, then stir it back through, leaving the rest fairly chunky (if you prefer it smoother or chunkier, adapt it to your preference). Remove from the heat and stir in the cream, then season to perfection and add a splash of water to make it a little thinner, if you wish. Serve topped with crumbled crispy bacon, smashed crackers and a sprinkling of parsley leaves (if using).

QUICK CHINESE WRAP

Whether you're making this for a lunch, snack or meal on the go, I love the fact that a humble everyday wrap can quickly be brought to life with lovely leftover chicken, some noodles, lettuce, and a hit of lime and hoisin to make it fantastic. I've given you the perfect quantities for one, but it's easy to scale this recipe up if you want to.

Serves 1
Total time: 10 minutes

416 calories

¾ oz fine rice noodles

1 large soft flour tortilla

¼ head of gem lettuce or heart of romaine

¼ carrot

2-inch piece of English cucumber

2 to 3 oz leftover cooked chicken

1 scallion

optional: ½ fresh red chile

1 heaping tablespoon hoisin sauce

½ lime

Snap the noodles into a small bowl, cover with boiling water and leave to rehydrate for 5 minutes, or until softened, then drain and refresh under cold water, draining again. Whether using a fresh or frozen tortilla, simply pop it into a microwave for 30 seconds, or in a dry frying pan on the stove, merely to heat it through and make it flexible (you don't want it crispy). Lay it flat on a clean work surface, place the lettuce leaves across the middle in a line and arrange the noodles on top.

Cut or scrape the watery core out of the cucumber, then coarsely grate it with the carrot on a box grater or cut them into matchsticks using good knife skills. Layer on top of the noodles, then shred or slice and add the chicken. Trim, finely slice and scatter over the scallions and chile (if using). Drizzle over the hoisin sauce, add a good squeeze of lime juice, then fold in the sides and roll up the wrap. Cut it in half and eat straight away, or wrap it in aluminum foil and pop it into the fridge for later.

The thing I love about this recipe is that it's a brilliant way to use up any scraps of leftover veg – radishes, celery, beets, white cabbage, fresh soft herbs – whatever you've got in the fridge. Also, you can swap out the chicken for any leftover meat, or even cooked shrimp. And, minus the chile, my kids have always loved these. Get creative and go for it.

CHICKEN & SPINACH CANNELLONI

LEFTOVER ...

One of the kings of comfort food has to be a hot, delicious, bubbling cannelloni, and this recipe is doing exactly what cannelloni was designed to do, which is to use up leftovers in a clear and concise way that costs very little and looks and tastes absolutely spanking – you're going to love this one.

Serves 6

Total time: 1 hour 10 minutes

498 calories

1 onion

olive oil

1 lb frozen spinach

2 tablespoons all-purpose flour

2 teaspoons English mustard

¾ cup reduced-fat (2%) milk

5 oz leftover cooked chicken

½ bunch of fresh basil (½ oz)

2 oz sharp Cheddar cheese

16 dried cannelloni tubes

2 cloves garlic

1–2 pinches of dried chili flakes

2 x 14-oz cans of diced tomatoes

extra virgin olive oil

Preheat the oven to 350°F. Peel and finely chop the onion and put it into a large saucepan on a medium heat with a lug of olive oil. Cook for 8 minutes, or until soft, stirring regularly and adding a splash of water, if needed, then stir in the spinach. Cook with a lid on for another 8 minutes to defrost, then stir in the flour and mustard. Gradually add the milk, stirring constantly for a couple of minutes, or until you have a nice creamy green sauce. Remove from the heat and season to perfection. Finely chop and add the chicken and basil leaves (reserving the stalks), then grate in half the Cheddar and mix well. A nice trick to get the filling into the cannelloni tubes easily is to transfer the mixture to a sandwich bag, snip off the corner and pipe the mixture into the tubes, or you can use a teaspoon, if you prefer. Once filled, place the tubes in one layer in a baking dish (roughly 10 x 12 inches). Wipe the saucepan out and return it to a medium heat.

Peel and finely chop the garlic and tender basil stalks, and put into the pan with a lug of olive oil to get lightly golden. Add the chili flakes, tip in the tomatoes and half a can's worth of water, bring to a boil for a couple of minutes, then season to perfection and pour over the pasta. Give the dish a loving shake to distribute the sauce evenly, grate over the remaining Cheddar, and bake at the bottom of the oven for around 30 minutes, or until golden and bubbling. Drizzle with a little extra virgin olive oil and serve.

JOINTING A
CHICKEN

Knowing how to joint a chicken is a really brilliant skill to have. Don't be scared – it's super simple, and you can buy a whole chicken for just a little bit more than the cost of two chicken breasts. Plus, you have the benefit of the drumsticks, thighs, wings and carcass to do many other delicious things with too, so it can be very economical. Please give it a go – all you need is a plastic cutting board (put a damp cloth underneath to secure it) and a sharp chopping knife, and you're away.

HERE'S WHAT TO DO:

1 Use your chopping knife to cut the skin between the breast and the leg.

2 Lever the leg away from the carcass, until the bone pops out of the socket.

3 Use the tip of the knife to cut the leg away from the carcass, angling the tip towards the carcass so you get as much meat on the leg as possible.

4 Use the heel of the knife to chop down through the joint of the wing.

5 Feel the breast bone down the center of the bird, then use the middle of the knife to cut vertically along it, to separate the breast from the bone.

6 Use the tip of your knife to cut between the breast meat and the carcass, slightly angling the knife towards the carcass in a stroking action.

7 Cut down between the breast and the carcass to remove the breast, angling the knife towards the carcass to ensure the breast is as meaty as possible.

8 Repeat all these steps for the other side of the bird. You can leave the legs whole, or cut them in half into thighs and drumsticks. To do this, use the middle of the knife to cut firmly in one confident movement through the joint at the natural bend of the leg. Save the carcass for making broth.

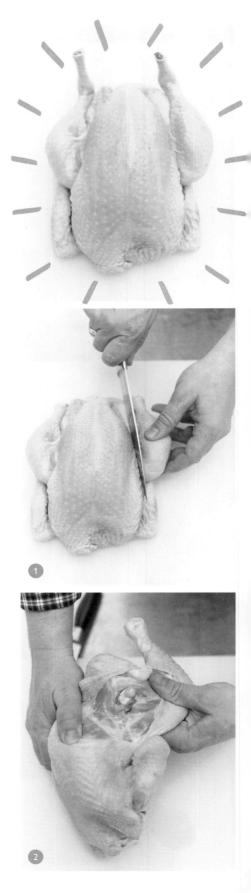

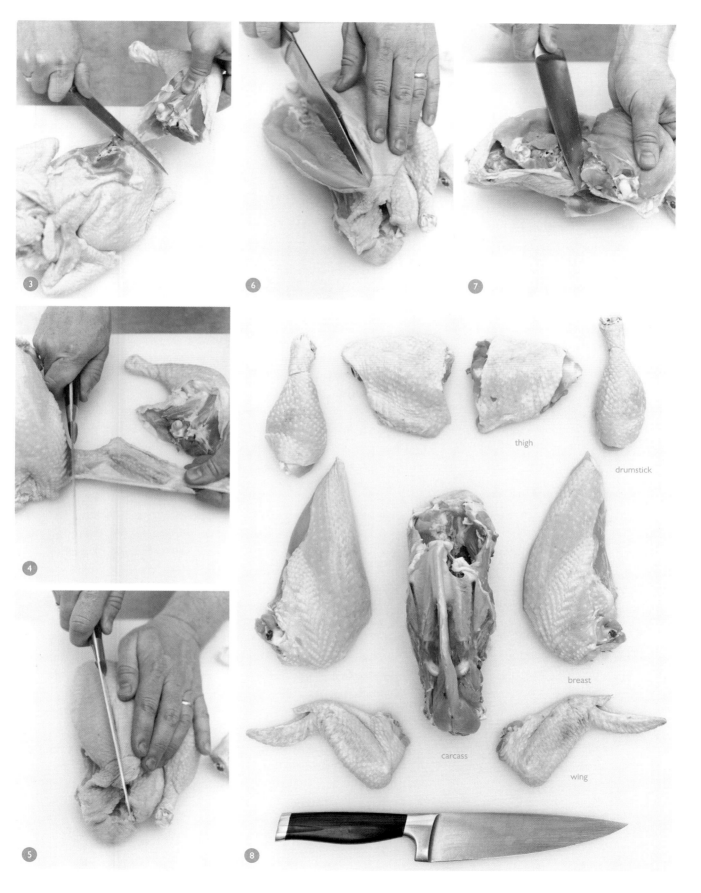

thigh

drumstick

breast

carcass

wing

JFC (JAMIE'S FRIED CHICKEN)

The love of chicken in a bucket everywhere is clear to see. I got a bucket for four people and it cost around $25 with a couple of sides, so I thought, let's give you a tasty, homemade version. I've upgraded the chicken, given you veggie sides in an exciting way, including a veg-packed slaw, and you should save about $5. Enjoy JFC.

Serves 4

Total time: 1 hour 35 minutes

893 calories

1 ¾ lbs sweet potatoes

olive oil

2 heaping tablespoons fine-ground cornmeal
  or polenta

1 x 4-lb whole chicken

1 heaping tablespoon Cajun seasoning

4 cloves garlic

2 carrots

1 apple

¼ head of white cabbage

1 small red onion

1 heaping teaspoon English mustard

2 tablespoons extra virgin olive oil

1 tablespoon white wine vinegar

3 heaping tablespoons fat-free
  plain yogurt

4 ½ oz ciabatta or stale bread

2 heaping tablespoons all-purpose flour

2 fresh corn on the cob (cut in half across
  the middle)

Preheat the oven to 375°F. Scrub the sweet potatoes clean, slice into wedges, toss in a pan with a little olive oil, 1 heaping tablespoon of cornmeal or polenta and a pinch of salt and pepper, then put aside. Cut up your chicken (see page 94 – you also want to split the legs into thighs and drumsticks for this recipe as described in step 8), then remove and discard the skin and lay the pieces on a large baking sheet. Add the remaining cornmeal or polenta, a good lug of olive oil and the Cajun seasoning to the sheet, squash over half the garlic through a garlic press, then toss and massage to coat the chicken. Place on the top shelf of the oven, pop the wedges underneath and cook for 20 minutes.

Meanwhile, coarsely grate the carrots, apple, cabbage and peeled onion in a food processor. Tip into a bowl and mix with the mustard, extra virgin olive oil, vinegar and yogurt, then season to perfection and put aside. Peel the remaining garlic and whiz in the food processor, then pulse in the bread and a good lug of olive oil until you have fine bread crumbs. Tip onto a tray. In a bowl, mix the flour with 4 tablespoons of water to make a paste.

When the time's up, remove the chicken from the oven, then carefully brush the pieces with the flour paste and use tongs to firmly press them in the bread crumbs until they're all evenly coated. Return the pan to the bottom of the oven, quickly turn the wedges and cook for a further 40 minutes, or until the chicken and sweet potatoes are golden and cooked through. Meanwhile, halve and grill the corn on a hot grill pan for around 15 minutes, or until hot through and charred, turning occasionally. Take everything to the table, get excited and dig in.

CHICKEN & CHORIZO PAELLA

I've made a few paellas in my time. The biggest one was for about 800 people in a village in Spain, and it was hard work but an incredible experience. The Spanish can be quite protective about what is and what isn't a paella, but at the same time, the spirit of their cooking has always been flexible to whatever meat, fish, seafood or game can be found. I've eaten and enjoyed many paellas, and I hope you like this humble, great-value expression of one.

Serves 4 to 6

Total time: 50 minutes

2 cloves garlic

1 onion

1 carrot

½ bunch of fresh Italian parsley (½ oz)

2 ½ oz chorizo

2 skinless boneless chicken thighs

olive oil

1 teaspoon sweet smoked paprika

1 red bell pepper

1 tablespoon tomato paste

1 chicken bouillon cube

10 oz paella or Valencia rice

¾ cup frozen peas

7 oz frozen peeled cooked shrimp

1 lemon

Peel and finely slice the garlic, then peel and roughly chop the onion and carrot. Finely chop the parsley stalks, then roughly chop the chorizo and chicken thighs. Put a lug of oil into a large lidded shallow casserole or paella pan on a medium heat, add the garlic, onion, carrot, parsley stalks, chorizo, chicken and paprika, and fry for around 5 minutes, stirring regularly. Seed and chop the pepper, then add to the pan for a further 5 minutes.

Stir through the tomato paste and crumble in the bouillon cube, then add the rice and stir for a couple of minutes so it starts to suck up all that lovely flavor. Pour in 3 cups of boiling water and add a pinch of salt and pepper. Pop the lid on and bring to a boil, then reduce to a simmer for 15 minutes, stirring regularly from the outside in and from the inside out, and adding a splash of water if needed. Stir in the peas and shrimp, replace the lid and cook for a further 5 minutes, or until hot through. Season to perfection, then chop the parsley leaves, scatter them over the paella and serve with lemon wedges on the side for squeezing over.

My advice here is simple: Delicious as this dish is, if you're feeling a bit flush, adding 6 mussels, 6 clams and any extra bits of fish you can afford is only going to make it even more of a celebration.

HIT 'N' RUN PANBAKED CHICKEN

Everyone needs a hit 'n' run recipe like this – it's the kind of fallback meal you can enjoy when prep time isn't on your side. It's simply a case of putting together a combination of ingredients that really love each other, then just tearing, mixing, marinating and baking. It's super quick to prepare, and you're letting the oven do all the work.

Serves 4

Total time: 1 hour 10 minutes

4 large ripe tomatoes

2 red onions

1 red bell pepper

1 yellow bell pepper

6 skinless boneless chicken thighs

4 cloves garlic

½ bunch of fresh thyme (½ oz)

1 teaspoon smoked paprika

2 tablespoons olive oil

2 tablespoons balsamic vinegar

Preheat the oven to 350°F. Quarter the tomatoes and place them in a large baking dish or roasting pan (roughly 10 x 12 inches). Peel the onions and cut into large wedges, then seed and roughly chop the peppers. Add all these to the pan along with the chicken thighs.

Squash the unpeeled garlic cloves with the back of your knife and add to the pan, then pick over the thyme leaves and sprinkle over the paprika. Add the oil, balsamic and a good pinch of salt and pepper. Toss everything together really well to coat, then spread across the pan, making sure the chicken isn't covered by the vegetables. Roast for around 1 hour, or until the chicken is golden and cooked through, turning and basting it a couple of times during cooking with the juices from the pan. Serve the panbake with a lovely green salad on the side. You could also buddy it up with a little rice, polenta or a loaf of crusty bread to mop up the juices.

Roasting garlic cloves whole in their skins makes them really sweet – don't waste that lovely soft flesh, squeeze it out and enjoy it!

STICKY CHICKEN CHINESE NOODLES

I love cooking super-easy meals like this that over-deliver on the taste front in a very short amount of time. This is a friendly play on some reliable old Anglo-Chinese flavors — sweet, sour and with a bit of fire from the chile, everyone's a winner. Feel free to use different shredded veg, and even a few sesame seeds, if you fancy.

Serves 4
Total time: 45 minutes

608 calories

4 skinless boneless chicken thighs

2 heaping teaspoons Chinese five-spice powder

olive oil

1 tablespoon honey

1 x 8-oz can of pineapple rings in juice

1 tablespoon reduced-sodium soy sauce

1 tablespoon white wine vinegar

1 heaping tablespoon cornstarch

4 nests of fine egg noodles

1 x 14-oz can of black beans

2 cloves garlic

1 onion

1 carrot

1–2 fresh red chiles

½ head of Napa cabbage

optional: ½ bunch of fresh cilantro (½ oz)

1 lime

Toss the chicken with half the five-spice and a pinch of salt and pepper, then flatten with your fist and leave for 15 minutes to let the flavors develop.

When the time's up, put the chicken into a large frying pan with a little oil and cook for 10 to 12 minutes, or until cooked through, turning regularly and drizzling with the honey for the last minute, to glaze. Remove the chicken to a plate, returning the pan to the heat.

Meanwhile, chop the pineapple rings into ¼-inch dice, put into a bowl with their juice, the soy sauce, vinegar and cornstarch, and mix together well. Cook the noodles in a pan of boiling salted water according to package instructions, then drain, reserving a little of the cooking water.

Drain and rinse the beans, then toss in a bowl with a tiny splash of oil and the remaining five-spice. Quickly wipe out the empty chicken pan with a ball of paper towel, then fry the beans on a high heat for about 5 minutes, or until crispy and burst. Remove from the pan and keep warm until needed, returning the pan to the heat. Peel and finely slice the garlic, onion and carrot along with the chile and cabbage and put into the empty bean pan with a lug of oil. Toss and cook for just 2 minutes, then add the pineapple and sauce, the noodles and a good swig of reserved cooking water and toss to coat. Taste and season to perfection with soy sauce, if needed.

Divide the noodles and crispy black beans between your plates. Slice the chicken and place on top, scatter with cilantro leaves (if using) and add a good squeeze of lime. Toss together, then dig in.

PUKKA YELLOW CURRY

"Pukka" is an Indian word for the real deal or authenticity, hence the name of this dish. It's not because I'm a cocky Essex boy, nor, as some not-so-nice journalists once said, because of my annoying "estuary accent" (whatever that means). Anyway, this curry is delicious – the meat falls off the bone, it's great value and it looks phenomenal.

Serves 4

Total time: 1 hour 15 minutes

2 onions

4 cloves garlic

1 thumb-sized piece of gingerroot

2 yellow bell peppers

1 chicken bouillon cube

1–2 fresh red chiles

½ bunch of fresh cilantro (½ oz)

1 teaspoon honey

1 level teaspoon ground turmeric

2 teaspoons curry powder

8 chicken drumsticks

olive oil

1 x 14-oz can of chickpeas

1 teaspoon tomato paste

1 mug (10 oz) of basmati rice

optional: fat-free plain yogurt, to serve

1 lemon

Peel the onions, garlic and ginger and seed the peppers. Put 1 onion, 1 pepper, the garlic and ginger into a food processor. Crumble in the bouillon cube and add the chile (seed it first, if you prefer a milder curry), the cilantro stalks, honey and spices, then blitz to a paste.

Place a large casserole pan on a medium-high heat and fry the chicken drumsticks (pull the skin off first, if you prefer) with a splash of oil for 10 minutes, or until golden, turning occasionally with tongs. Remove the chicken to a plate, leaving the pan on the heat. Roughly chop the remaining onion and pepper and add to the pan to cook for a few minutes, then tip in the paste and let it cook down for around 5 minutes. Pour in 2 cups of boiling water. Drain the chickpeas and add along with the tomato paste and a pinch of salt and pepper, then stir well. Return the chicken to the pan, pop the lid on, reduce the heat and simmer gently for around 45 minutes, or until the sauce darkens and thickens.

With 15 minutes to go, put 1 mug of rice and 2 mugs of boiling water into a saucepan with a pinch of salt and simmer with the lid on for 12 minutes, or until all the liquid has been absorbed. Serve the curry in the middle of the table with a few dollops of yogurt (if using) and a scattering of cilantro leaves, with lemon wedges for squeezing over and the fluffy rice on the side.

CHICKEN WINGS GANGNAM-STYLE

I love this dish – it's definitely finger-licking good. It's inspired by Korean and Chinese flavors and that crazy song that all my kids love (I reckon by calling a dish after something they love you've got more chance of them eating it). Anyway, from kids to adults, this is a solid recipe to give you tender, sweet wing meat with a beautiful sticky glaze. With eggy rice on the side it's a great combo and happy, messy eating – not one for a first date!

Serves 4

Total time: 1 hour 40 minutes

12 chicken wings

2 heaping teaspoons Chinese five-spice powder

7 oz brown rice

1 thumb-sized piece of gingerroot

2 tablespoons tomato ketchup

1 tablespoon reduced-sodium soy sauce

1 tablespoon honey

1 tablespoon raw sesame seeds

2 cloves garlic

1–2 fresh red chiles

2 bok choy

Asian sesame oil

1 large egg

Preheat the oven to 350°F. Stretch out the chicken wings, cut the bingo wings–type skin in the middle, then pop out any joints, if you can, to make them straight (you can poke wooden skewers through the wings to hold them like this, if you like). Place the wings in a snug-fitting roasting pan (roughly 10 x 12 inches), scatter over the five-spice and a good pinch of salt and toss together until evenly coated. Cover with aluminum foil and cook for around 50 minutes, or until tender.

Meanwhile, cook the rice according to package instructions, then drain, spread out on a tray and leave to cool. Peel the ginger, finely grate into a small bowl and mix with the ketchup, soy sauce and honey to make a glaze. When the time's up, remove the foil from the tray, then coat the chicken wings with some of the glaze, and either return them to the oven or pop them under a medium broiler (and watch them like a hawk) for a final 30 minutes, or until golden and gnarly, turning and brushing with more glaze every 5 to 10 minutes to use it all up and make them super sticky. Evenly sprinkle over the sesame seeds from a height after adding your last bit of glaze.

When the wings are nearly ready, peel and slice the garlic with the chile and bok choy, then put them into a large frying pan or wok on a medium heat with a lug of oil. Get them lightly golden, keeping them moving around the pan, then add the rice and let it heat through. Transfer the pan of wings to the stove, remove the wings to one side and pour ¾ cup of water into the pan. Boil and simmer for 5 minutes, scraping up all the sticky bits from the bottom of the pan, then skim any fat off the surface and mix the sauce into the rice. Push the rice to one side of the pan and crack the egg into the gap. Stir it around so it starts to scramble and cook, then toss through the rice. Season to perfection and serve with the sticky chicken wings, right away.

MEXICAN CAESAR SALAD

Caesar is a classic salad — simple chicken, crunchy leaves and a dressing with attitude. This version has had a fight with some tasty Mexican flavors and gained a silky smooth, delicious avocado dressing, which is the most divine color. I think it moves it on to the next level, lightens it up and keeps people interested. Give it a go.

Serves 4

Total time: 40 minutes

338 calories

2 x 7-oz skinless boneless chicken breasts

1 pinch of cayenne pepper

2 pinches of dried oregano

olive oil

1 head of romaine lettuce

1 head of gem lettuce or heart of romaine

8 ripe cherry or grape tomatoes

¼ English cucumber

1 ripe avocado

1 ½ oz Parmesan cheese

½ clove garlic

2 anchovy fillets

4 tablespoons fat-free plain yogurt

1 lemon

Worcestershire sauce

3 tablespoons extra virgin olive oil

4 rashers of smoked bacon

1 small loaf of brown bread, to serve

On a large sheet of parchment paper, toss the chicken with a pinch each of salt, pepper, cayenne and oregano, and a little olive oil. Fold over the paper, then bash and flatten the chicken to ¾ inch thick with a rolling pin. Put a grill pan on a high heat to get nice and hot.

Meanwhile, trim then slice the bases of the lettuces, break the leaves apart, and place in a big bowl. Halve or quarter the tomatoes and erratically slice the cucumber (I'm loving my crinkle-cut knife — you should get one!), and add both to the bowl. Squeeze the avocado flesh into a blender, finely grate in half the Parmesan and add the peeled garlic, anchovies, yogurt, the juice from the lemon, a few drops of Worcestershire sauce and the extra virgin olive oil. Whiz until smooth, then season to perfection — you want it slightly too acidic, so add extra lemon juice, if needed.

Grill the chicken for 3 to 4 minutes on each side, and the bacon for a couple of minutes on each side, or until it's all nicely charred, then remove. Add half the dressing to the bowl of salad and toss well to coat, then tip onto a nice serving platter. Slice the chicken and arrange on top of the salad with the bacon, then drizzle over the remaining dressing. Grate over the remaining Parmesan, sprinkle with the rest of the oregano from a height, then serve with a loaf of warm crusty bread.

If you've got any fresh mint, cilantro or Italian parsley in the fridge or growing on your windowsill, add a handful of leaves to the avocado dressing when you blitz it to add even more flavor.

DELICIOUS CHICKEN LIVER BOLOGNESE

Chicken livers are fantastic value. You can pick them up at the supermarket or the butcher's – they add the most wonderful flavor, and simply braised in this delicious ragù, with lentils to add a bit of bulk, they will give you a rustic, Bolognese-style sauce. It's sweet, it's tender and around spaghetti it's just wonderful.

Serves 6

Total time: 1 hour 10 minutes

454 calories

8 oz chicken livers

1 red onion

1 carrot

2 cloves garlic

3 ½ oz button mushrooms

2 sprigs of fresh rosemary

1 teaspoon fennel seeds

½ teaspoon dried chili flakes

optional: a few sprigs of fresh Italian parsley

2 rashers of smoked bacon

olive oil

1 x 19-oz can of lentils

2 tablespoons tomato paste

3 tablespoons balsamic vinegar

1 chicken bouillon cube

17 oz dried spaghetti

Parmesan cheese, to serve

Soak the livers in a bowl of water for a few minutes. Meanwhile, peel the onion, carrot and garlic, then pulse in a food processor with the mushrooms, rosemary leaves, fennel seeds, chili flakes and parsley stalks (if using), until finely chopped. Finely slice the bacon and put it into a large saucepan on a medium heat with a good lug of oil. Add the pulsed mixture from the processor to the pan and cook for around 15 minutes, or until softened, stirring occasionally and adding a splash of water to help it along, if needed.

Drain the chicken livers, then pulse in the food processor until finely chopped. Use a spatula to scrape them into the veg pan, then fry and break up for a couple of minutes. Drain, rinse and add the lentils, followed by the tomato paste and vinegar. Crumble in the bouillon cube and add 2 ¾ cups of boiling water (if you've got any leftover chicken broth, use that here instead to add great extra flavor). Reduce to a low heat and simmer gently for 40 minutes. With 15 minutes to go, finely chop the parsley leaves (if using). Cook the pasta in a large saucepan of boiling salted water according to package instructions, then drain, reserving a cupful of cooking water.

Season the sauce to perfection, then tip in the pasta and toss together, loosening with a splash of cooking water, if needed. Sprinkle over the chopped parsley, finely grate over a little Parmesan, toss and serve.

MY JEWISH PENICILLIN
OMELET RIBBONS

This brilliant recipe is called "Jewish penicillin" because with broth, veg and noodles, it's a real pick-me-up. There are loads of variations of this recipe out there, but this is my current comforting favorite. Of course, you can use any seasonal veg or any frozen stuff you've got in the freezer to bulk this out, and the super-special twist here is the fantastic rustic omelet noodles – I learnt how to make them in Japan and they really work a treat.

Serves 6
Total time: 1 hour 30 minutes

 310 calories

1 onion

1 carrot

1 potato

1 leek

olive oil

1 chicken bouillon cube

4 skinless chicken thighs, bone in

½ cup pearl barley

2 large eggs

½ head of Savoy cabbage

7 oz frozen broccoli florets

3 ½ oz fine rice noodles

Peel and roughly chop the onion, carrot, potato and leek and put into a large saucepan on a medium heat with a lug of oil. Cook for 15 minutes, or until soft but not colored, stirring occasionally. Crumble in the bouillon cube, then add the chicken thighs, pearl barley and 10 cups of boiling water (or use leftover chicken broth, if you have it). Stir well and leave to simmer for around 45 minutes with the lid on.

Meanwhile, beat the eggs in a bowl with a few tablespoons of water to thin them out. Place a small non-stick frying pan on a medium heat with a splash of oil, then make 3 or 4 really thin pancake-style omelets, without letting them get any color. Cool, roll up and slice.

Trim and shred the cabbage, discarding the core, and add to the soup with the broccoli. Simmer for 5 minutes while you pull out the chicken thighs, shred the meat off the bone and put it back into the soup, discarding the bones. Season the soup to perfection, then simply add your rice noodles, off the heat, and serve 5 minutes later when they're hydrated. Sprinkle over the omelet noodles at the last minute before serving – delicious.

If you've got some fresh parsley in the fridge, chop a few leaves and add to your egg mixture to bring a bit of fragrant flavor to the omelet noodles.

I've written this recipe using 4 humble chicken thighs, which give great flavor and can be easily shredded into the soup, but it will work just as well using leftover cooked chicken from your Sunday roast.

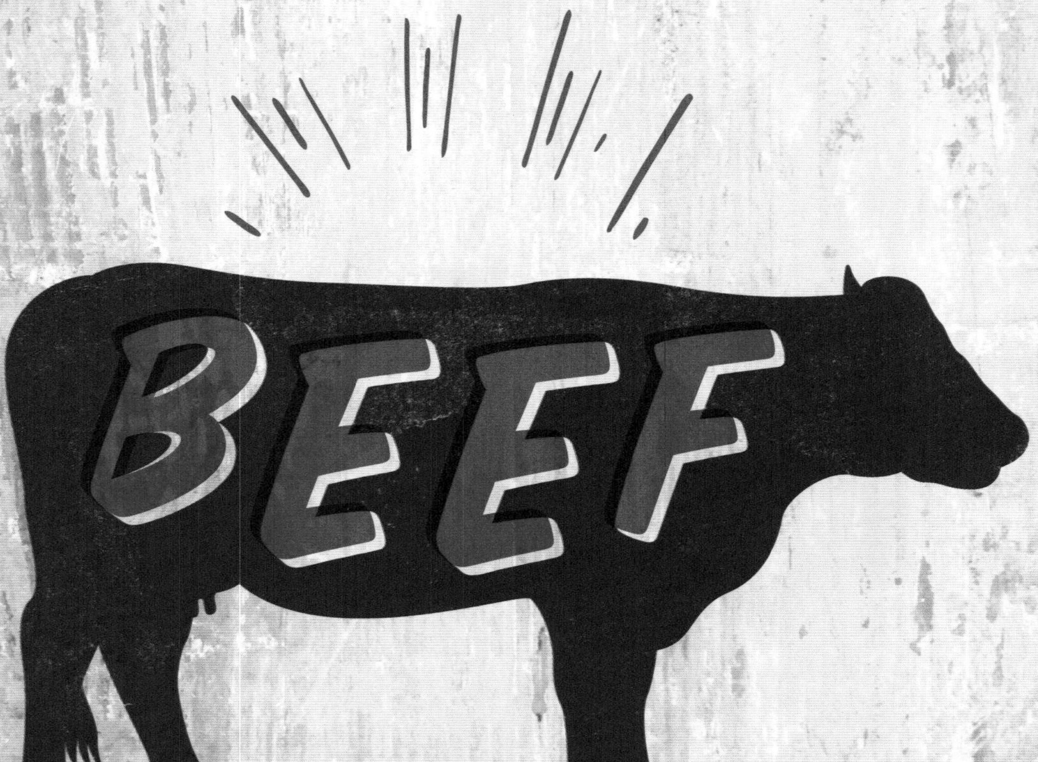
BEEF

• BEEF RECIPES •

We all love beef, but sadly it can be incredibly expensive to buy, so this chapter is all about me holding your hand and guiding you through some of the really tasty cheaper cuts. I found it very exciting writing these recipes, and I hope they'll give you a good appreciation of the whole animal, not just those more costly, well-known cuts. Veering away from tradition, I've given you a brisket roast dinner, which is phenomenal and provides outrageous leftovers for future meals. I've also used a variety of cheaper cuts, including secret steaks that will make shopping at the butcher's way more fun. It's always good to buy beef from the country that you live in, and if possible, go for grass-fed cattle, which are healthier animals that in turn will nourish you in a much more healthy way.

MOTHERSHIP SUNDAY ROAST BRISKET

Roast beef is the ultimate treat, but brisket is your thrifty friend — it's a forgiving, wonderful cut of beef with amazing flavor, whether you go for juicy, carvable slices or shreds of beautiful pulled meat. You can get a 2-lb piece from the supermarket, but it's best to get 4 lbs from your butcher and make amazing things out of the leftovers.

Serves 6 plus leftovers
Total time: 4 ½ to 5 ½ hours

619 calories

4-lb piece of beef brisket

olive oil

2 large onions

2 teaspoons English mustard

1 bunch of fresh rosemary (1 oz)

5 lbs potatoes

1 lb carrots

1 rutabaga

1 knob of unsalted butter

1 cup all-purpose flour

1 tablespoon blackcurrant jam

2 tablespoons red wine vinegar

vegetable oil

2 large eggs

⅓ cup reduced-fat (2%) milk

> If you're not going to use all the leftover brisket within 2 or 3 days, simply portion it up and freeze for making meals in future weeks. Defrost in the fridge for 24 hours before cooking.

Preheat the oven to 325°F. Place a large casserole pan (12 inches in diameter) on a high heat. Season the brisket well with salt and pepper and brown it in the hot pan with a lug of olive oil while you peel and slice the onions. Turn the heat off and place the onions underneath the brisket. Spread the fat side of the meat with the mustard and strip over most of the rosemary leaves. Protect the meat with a wet piece of parchment paper, then tightly cover the pan with a double layer of aluminum foil and cook for around 4 hours for carvable meat, or around 5 for pulled meat. Check it halfway and add a splash of water, if needed, sealing the foil back securely.

Meanwhile, peel the potatoes, halving any larger ones, and parboil in a large saucepan of boiling salted water for 12 minutes. Drain and shake to fluff up, then tip into a roasting pan with a lug of olive oil, a pinch of salt and pepper and the remaining rosemary leaves, and toss to coat. Place in the oven below the brisket for the final 1 ½ hours. Peel and roughly chop the carrots and rutabaga. Cook in a pan of boiling salted water for 20 minutes, or until soft, then drain. Return to the pan, mash with the butter, season to perfection and keep warm.

Remove the brisket and potatoes from the oven, transfer to a board and cover, then turn the oven to full whack (495°F). Put the pan on a medium heat on the stove and stir in 2 tablespoons of flour. Stir in the jam, vinegar, 1 ⅔ cups of boiling water and any resting juices, then simmer until you're happy with the consistency. Meanwhile, put a 12-cup shallow bun pan into the oven with a little vegetable oil in each compartment, to get hot. Put a heaping ¾ cup of flour into a pitcher with a pinch of salt, whisk in the eggs, then gradually add the milk until you have a smooth batter. Remove the pan from the oven, then quickly and carefully fill each compartment three-quarters full with batter and return to the oven for 10 minutes, or until puffed up and golden. Carve up or pull apart half the brisket, saving half for leftovers. Serve everything in the middle of the table with seasonal greens and all your usual trimmings.

BEEF RENDANG

Rendang is a wonderfully perfumed, thick, spiced stew from Indonesia and is often touted as one of the tastiest foods in the world. It normally takes hours of stirring and vigilant care, but of course using leftover brisket means it can be made in a reasonably short time, with equally tender, beautiful results.

Serves 6
Total time: 40 minutes

563 calories

2 onions

2 large thumb-sized pieces of gingerroot

4 cloves garlic

1 bunch of fresh cilantro (1 oz)

1–2 fresh red chiles

1 teaspoon ground turmeric

½ teaspoon ground cinnamon

olive oil

16 oz leftover cooked brisket

1 x 14-oz can of light coconut milk

optional: leftover beef gravy

17 oz basmati rice

chapattis or flatbreads, to serve

1 lime, to serve

fat-free plain yogurt, to serve

Peel the onions, ginger and garlic, put into a food processor with the cilantro stalks, chile, turmeric and cinnamon, and blitz into a paste. Put a lug of oil into a large frying pan on a low heat, then scrape in the paste and fry for around 15 minutes, or until lightly golden, stirring occasionally.

Chop or roughly shred the brisket and stir it into the pan, then add the coconut milk, half a can's worth of water (if you've got any leftover gravy from the mothership recipe, add that here too), and a pinch of salt and pepper. Bring to a boil, then reduce to a simmer for a further 10 to 15 minutes, or until thickened and reduced, stirring occasionally. Meanwhile, cook the rice according to package instructions with a pinch of salt. Simply heat the chapattis through in a dry pan, or warm them in the microwave (you want them to be flexible).

Finely grate the lime zest into the curry and squeeze in half the juice, then cut the remaining half into wedges. Season the rendang to perfection, then serve with the fluffy rice and a sprinkling of cilantro leaves, with the lime wedges, yogurt and chapattis on the side. Absolute heaven.

> You can definitely use storebought chapattis here, but if you fancy making your own, then check out the simple recipe on page 58.

SPICED BEEF TAGINE

LEFTOVER...

A rich, spiced tagine is definitely one of the ultimate stews, and served with couscous it's a total pleasure to eat. What's great about this recipe is that it takes your leftover brisket and surrounds it with flavors that really can't go wrong, giving you sweetness, spice and excitement. This is proper comfort food with a difference.

Serves 6

Total time: 1 hour

485 calories

2 red onions

2 oz mixed olives, with pits

2 ½ oz soft dried apricots

2 cloves garlic

olive oil

1 heaping tablespoon garam masala

2 teaspoons ground cumin

½ level teaspoon dried chili flakes

2 potatoes

2 large ripe tomatoes

1 x 14-oz can of chickpeas

14 oz leftover cooked brisket

1 beef bouillon cube

optional: leftover beef gravy

1 ⅓ cups couscous

1 orange

2 carrots

½ bunch of fresh mint (½ oz)

extra virgin olive oil

optional: balsamic vinegar

fat-free plain yogurt, to serve

Peel the onions, tear the pits out of the olives, then roughly chop both with the apricots. Peel and finely chop the garlic, then put all of it into a casserole pan on a medium heat with a lug of olive oil, the garam masala, cumin and chili flakes. Cook for about 15 minutes, or until soft, stirring regularly and adding splashes of water to stop it sticking, if needed.

Roughly chop the potatoes (skin on) and tomatoes, and add to the pan along with the chickpeas (juice and all). Cut the meat into 1-inch chunks and add to the pan, then crumble in the bouillon cube and add 1 cup of boiling water (if you've got some leftover gravy from the mothership recipe, add that here too – it'll give a wicked depth of flavor). Bring to a boil, then simmer with the lid on for 20 to 25 minutes, or until the potatoes are cooked through, adding splashes of water to loosen, if needed.

Meanwhile, pop the couscous into a bowl, just cover with boiling water, put a plate on top and leave for 10 minutes to do its thing. Top and tail the orange, then use a knife to peel and segment it onto a board. Peel and coarsely grate the carrots, pick over the mint leaves and toss everything on the board together, squeezing over any juice from the leftover central part of the orange. Add a lug of extra virgin olive oil and a pinch of salt and pepper, then toss again. Fluff up your couscous, season to perfection, then tip onto a large platter. Season the tagine (sometimes I add a swig of balsamic vinegar to taste) and spoon it over the couscous. Drizzle with yogurt, then pile the shredded carrot, mint and orange salad in the center.

If you've got ras el hanout in your pantry, use that instead of garam masala to add a bit of extra authenticity on the flavor front.

PULLED BEEF SALAD
KICK-ASS CROUTONS

LEFTOVER...

I love a good, simple, confident salad — light crunchy leaves, slaps of heat from the chile, really tasty hot croutons and, very importantly, a kick-ass but subtle blue cheese dressing that will make this small amount of lovely leftover meat go such a long way. And if in doubt, just chuck it in a wrap or pita to make it even more gorgeous.

Serves 6

Total time: 30 minutes

427 calories

2 ½ oz blue cheese

5 tablespoons olive oil

3 tablespoons cider or white wine vinegar

3 teaspoons grainy mustard

1 French baguette

optional: leftover beef gravy

2 heads of bibb lettuce

½ bunch of fresh mint (½ oz)

2 apples or pears (or 1 of each)

8 oz leftover cooked brisket

1 fresh red chile

Preheat the oven to 350°F. Crumble the blue cheese into a blender and add the oil, vinegar, mustard and a pinch of pepper. Whiz until smooth, then loosen with a good splash of water, if needed — you want it to be thick enough to just coat the back of a spoon.

Tear the bread into rough 1-inch chunks and scatter over a large roasting pan. Drizzle over one-third of the blue cheese dressing and toss together (if you've got any leftover gravy from the mothership recipe, a couple of spoonfuls drizzled over the croutons as well will add great extra flavor), then roast in one layer for 10 to 15 minutes, or until golden and crunchy, turning halfway.

Break the lettuce leaves apart into a large bowl, then pick in the mint leaves. Cut your apples and/or pears into chunky matchsticks (I'm loving my crinkle-cut knife — you should get one!) and add to the bowl. Place a large saucepan over a high heat, tear or shred in the brisket and toss and dry-fry for a couple of minutes to warm through, then add to the salad bowl. Drizzle over the remaining dressing and toss everything together. Tip onto a large platter or divide between your plates, scatter over the croutons, finely slice the chile and sprinkle over the top, then tuck in.

If you want to make this into a more creamy dressing, simply replace 2 tablespoons of oil with 2 heaping tablespoons of fat-free plain yogurt. Any avocados you've got spare will be delicious chopped into chunks and added into the salad mix too.

HUMBLE BRISKET STEW – 4 WAYS

This is a super-tasty brisket stew, served my four favorite easy ways – pick the one you like best and enjoy!

Peel and roughly chop 2 onions and 4 carrots and put them into a large saucepan on a low heat with a lug of olive oil. Pick and chop the leaves from 2 sprigs of fresh rosemary and add to the pan along with 2 fresh bay leaves. Cook for around 15 minutes with the lid ajar, or until softened, stirring occasionally. Stir in 1 heaping tablespoon of all-purpose flour, then add 1 tablespoon each of tomato paste, grainy mustard and Worcestershire sauce. Crumble in 1 beef bouillon cube and pour in 2 ½ cups of boiling water. Stir through ½ cup of pearl barley, halve and add 8 oz of cremini mushrooms, along with 10 oz of sliced leftover cooked brisket, then leave to tick away for around 1 hour, or until the pearl barley is cooked and the stew is dark and sticky, stirring occasionally and adding splashes of water to loosen, if needed. If turning into a hotpot, or serving with yorkies or jacket spuds, you can start the recipes below while your stew is cooking. Season the stew to perfection and serve with some seasonal greens.

BRISKET STEW & YORKIES

714 calories

Serves 6

Total time: 1 hour 30 minutes including stew

Preheat the oven to 495°F. Put a 12-cup muffin pan into the oven with a little vegetable oil in each of the compartments, to get hot. Put 1 ⅓ cups of all-purpose flour into a pitcher with a pinch of salt, whisk in 4 large eggs, then gradually add ¾ cup reduced-fat (2%) milk until you have a smooth batter. Remove the muffin pan from the oven, then quickly and carefully fill the compartments three-quarters full with batter and return to the oven to cook for 25 minutes, or until puffed up and golden. Serve with your hot stew.

BRISKET HOTPOT

596 calories

Serves 6

Total time: 1 hour 40 minutes including stew

Preheat the oven to 375°F. While your stew is simmering, slice 16 oz of potatoes (skin on), either by hand with good knife skills or ⅛ inch thick on a mandolin (use the guard!). Take the stew off the heat 30 minutes before the time's up, season to perfection and tip into a baking dish (roughly 10 x 12 inches). Arrange the potatoes in a fan across the top, drizzle with a little olive oil and a pinch of salt and pepper, and cook in the oven for 40 minutes, or until golden, crispy and cooked through.

BRISKET STEW & JACKET SPUDS

719 calories

Serves 6

Total time: 1 hour 30 minutes including stew

Preheat the oven to 375°F. Wash 6 baking potatoes and stab all over with a fork. Lightly season with salt and pepper and bake for around 1 hour, or until crisp on the outside and fluffy in the middle. Score a criss-cross in the top of the potatoes, squeeze them at the base to bust them open, then plate up, spoon the hot brisket stew over the top and tuck in.

BRISKET PUFF PASTRY PIE

893 calories

Serves 6

Total time: 2 hours 10 minutes including stew

Preheat the oven to 375°F. Transfer the stew to a baking dish (roughly 10 x 12 inches) and eggwash the sides. On a flour-dusted surface, roll out 10 oz of puff pastry until slightly bigger than the dish, then place on top. Pinch the edges to seal, score a cross in the middle, eggwash and bake for 30 minutes (40 minutes if the stew is cold), or until golden and hot through.

BEEF NOODLE SOUP

You've got to love a bowl of beef noodle soup – it's therapeutic, full of goodness and a great way to embrace green veg in a really exciting dish to enjoy alongside our tender, braised brisket. This recipe works a treat whether you're using leftover slices of beef like I've done here, or if you've got lovely pulled meat. Delicious!

Serves 4

Total time: 50 minutes

2 thumb-sized pieces of gingerroot

4 cloves garlic

1–2 fresh red chiles

olive oil

optional: 2 star anise

½ bunch of fresh cilantro (½ oz)

2 beef bouillon cubes

11 oz medium rice noodles

10 oz leftover cooked brisket

2 tablespoons BBQ sauce

1 head of Napa cabbage

3 ½ oz frozen broccoli florets

⅓ cup frozen peas

2 oz beansprouts

optional: reduced-sodium soy sauce

2 scallions

1 lime

Peel, break and bust the ginger, along with the unpeeled garlic and 1 chile, on a board with a rolling pin, then put into a large saucepan on a low heat with a lug of oil for around 15 minutes, or until golden brown, stirring regularly. Remove the pan from the heat, carefully take out and finely slice the ginger and chile, and squeeze the garlic cloves out of their skins. Return it all to the pan with the star anise (if using), then finely slice the cilantro stalks and add. Put the pan back on the heat, crumble in the bouillon cubes, pour in 8 cups of water and bring to a boil, then reduce to a simmer for 30 minutes.

Meanwhile, put the noodles into a bowl, cover with boiling water and soak for 15 minutes, or until tender, moving them about with tongs every now and then to separate. Refresh under cold water and drain. Slice up or roughly shred the brisket, rub with half the BBQ sauce, and put aside. Finely slice the bottom quarter of the Napa cabbage and break apart the rest of the leaves. When the time's up on the broth, place a grill pan on a high heat. Once screaming hot, add the brisket, turning when gnarly and bar-marked, and basting a few times with the remaining BBQ sauce (invest time here and you'll reap the rewards). Meanwhile, add the broccoli to the broth for a minute or two, followed by the sliced Napa cabbage, peas, noodles and beansprouts for a couple more minutes, then season the broth to perfection with soy sauce, if needed.

Divide the noodles, veg broth and raw Napa cabbage leaves between four bowls, then top with the gnarly brisket. Trim and finely slice the scallions and any remaining chile, then scatter over the bowls with the cilantro leaves. Serve with lime wedges for squeezing over.

KOREAN STIR-FRIED RICE

When I went to Korea, everyone was eating a really popular dish called *bibimbap*. It's basically varying combinations of greens, rice, egg, condiments, sauces and pickles that you bring together yourself at the table. I took that inspiration and injected it into this stir-fried beef and rice dish with lots of color, flavor and texture. If you're lucky, you'll get crispy rice at the edges and fluffy rice in the middle. Serve with hot chili sauce for an added kick.

Serves 4

Total time: 40 minutes

589 calories

1 mug (10 oz) of brown or white basmati rice

7 oz leftover cooked brisket

2 tablespoons BBQ sauce

2 tablespoons hot chili sauce

reduced-sodium soy sauce

2 tablespoons raw sesame seeds

2 cloves garlic

1 fresh red chile

5 oz button mushrooms

Asian sesame oil

½ head of Savoy cabbage

5 large eggs

Cook the rice according to package instructions in a large saucepan with a pinch of salt. Meanwhile, roughly shred the beef and mix well in a bowl with the BBQ and chili sauces and 1 tablespoon of soy sauce. Set aside.

Toast the sesame seeds in a large shallow saucepan on a medium heat for 1 minute, then tip out and put aside, keeping the pan to use again. About 5 minutes before the rice is ready, peel the garlic, finely slice it with the chile and put into the large pan with the mushrooms and 2 tablespoons of oil to fry for a minute. Add the beef and the marinade to the pan to glaze while you shred the cabbage (discarding the core). When the beef is sticky and golden, add the cabbage to the pan and cook for 4 to 5 minutes, or until cooked down, tossing occasionally.

Drain the rice and add to the pan with a little swig of soy sauce, then crack in one of the eggs and stir really well. Reduce the heat, then press the rice down at the sides to encourage crispy bits while you poach the remaining eggs — wipe out the pan you cooked the rice in and poach the eggs in simmering water for 2 to 4 minutes, depending on how you like them cooked. Serve the rice straight from the pan with the poached eggs on top. Bust open the eggs, scatter over the toasted sesame seeds and drizzle with extra chili sauce, if you dare.

SLOPPY BRISKET PO' BOY

LEFTOVER...

Everyone's got to try a po' boy sarnie — it has the potential to be the ultimate hot sandwich. Filled with anything from crispy shrimp to, in this case, juicy meat in delicious gravy that seeps through the bread and works incredibly well with pickles and mustard, it's a wicked sandwich hailing from good old Louisiana in the US of A. In fact, it's so good it makes me drool just thinking about it. Give this one a go and you won't look back.

Serves 4
Total time: 15 minutes

411 calories

⅓ cup leftover beef gravy

10 oz leftover cooked brisket

1 ciabatta loaf

2 dill pickles

4 pickled onions

1 fresh red chile

¼ head of iceberg lettuce

optional: 1 cup sprouted cress

1 tablespoon English mustard

Preheat the oven to 350°F. Heat the leftover gravy from the mothership recipe in a saucepan or roasting pan on a low heat with enough boiling water to loosen, stirring occasionally, then either slice or pull apart the brisket and add it to the gravy for a few minutes. Meanwhile, place the ciabatta in the oven for 5 minutes to warm through.

Once warm, cut the ciabatta in half lengthways (so you end up with two wide halves) and spoon the leftover meat and as much gravy as you like over the base. Slice up the dill pickles, pickled onions and chile and dot over the top. Shred up and pile the lettuce and some sprouted cress (if using) on top for a bit of crunch, then spread the mustard onto the top side of the ciabatta. Sandwich together, slice into four and shove it in your gob. Feel free to dip your sandwich in any extra leftover gravy — it's not going to be pretty or glamorous, and it will dribble all down your arms, but you'll have a smile bigger than Pac-Man. I like to find a quiet corner, put a towel over my head and enjoy it.

This style of sarnie works really well with pretty much any leftover meat and, of course, can be done in individual buns if you prefer.

KNOW YOUR...
BUTCHER

Making a point of finding a good local butcher and getting to know them on first-name terms is an investment for life. If you're a regular, and you talk to them about the occasion you're cooking for, or tell them that you've only got a certain amount of money to feed a set number of people, I assure you they will help you shop smart, cook clever and waste less. Supermarkets are very convenient, but it's hard for any of them to compare to a passionate local butcher. However, I think it's fair to say some are better than others, so my mate and master butcher John Stenton has given me advice on how to spot a great butcher. Just follow these tips:

1 Good butchers take pride in their display — meat should be kept refreshed and not left sitting in pools of blood.

2 Butchers should know exactly where all the meat comes from, the breeds of the animals and the standards and welfare they were raised in, so please always ask these questions — it's perfectly normal to do so.

3 The meat in the butcher's should largely be from the country you're in, and ideally from farms in the local area.

4 A great gauge is to ask about sausages! Good butchers take pride in making their own and will delight in telling you what's in them and when they were made. They should have been made within the last 24 hours, or that same day, have a high meat content and use natural casings. Again, it's fine to ask all these questions.

5 Butchers should happily make ground meat to order, so you know what's in it and can get the amount you need.

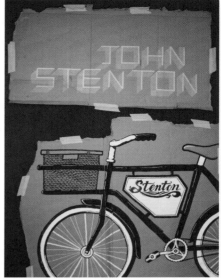

SHOP SMART

Stenton Family Butchers, 55 Aldensley Road, Hammersmith, London, UK, W6 0DH

MEXICAN BEEF CHILI

I absolutely adore cooking dishes like this with a nice hunk of meat on the bone, and shank is great value. You get tender, sweet meat, and the marrow from the bone gives the sauce great flavor. This will completely reset your standards of what a really good chili is, and it also makes wicked party food if you're feeding a crowd.

Serves 8
Total time: 5 hours 30 minutes

327 calories

2 red onions

4 cloves garlic

2 fresh red chiles

1 bunch of fresh cilantro (1 oz)

olive oil

2 teaspoons ground cumin

2 teaspoons smoked paprika

2 teaspoons ground cinnamon

2 fresh bay leaves

2 x 14-oz cans of diced tomatoes

2 lbs beef shank, bone in, sinew removed

1 x 14-oz can of cannellini beans

1 green bell pepper

4 scallions

5 oz cherry or grape tomatoes

extra virgin olive oil

white wine vinegar

optional: fat-free plain yogurt, to serve

Preheat the oven to 325°F. Peel and finely chop the onions and garlic with the chiles and cilantro stalks, then put into a large casserole pan on a medium heat with a good lug of olive oil. Add all the spices and the bay leaves and cook for 15 minutes, stirring regularly, and adding a splash or two of water to stop it sticking, if needed.

Pour in the canned tomatoes and two cans' worth of water and bring to a boil while you rub the meat all over with salt, pepper and olive oil. Pop the meat into the sauce, cover with a lid, then transfer to the oven to cook for 5 hours, stirring halfway and adding a good splash of water to loosen, if needed. Twenty minutes before the end, drain the beans and stir through, adding a splash of juice from the can if the chili looks a bit dry.

Meanwhile, seed the pepper, trim the scallions, then chop with the cherry or grape tomatoes and most of the cilantro leaves. Season to perfection and toss with a lug of extra virgin olive oil and a swig of vinegar to make a quick salsa. When the meat is falling apart and the chili is thick and delicious, shake the marrow out of the bone and stir it back through the chili. Season to perfection again, if needed, then sprinkle over the remaining cilantro leaves and serve with the salsa, and a dollop of yogurt, if you like. Delicious with grilled corn on the cob and baked sweet potatoes on the side.

MINCE & ONION PIE
CREAM CHEESE PASTRY

Many generations have been brought up on pies like this. I didn't want to steer too far from tradition, so I've kept this one very humble and beautiful – it's all about a simple filling and a damn good pastry recipe. Serve with some steamed seasonal greens and a spoonful of mashed potato, and you know everything will be all right . . .

Serves 6

Total time: 1 hour 40 minutes

 628 calories

1 ¼ lbs ground beef

olive oil

3 large red onions

8 sprigs of fresh thyme

1 ½ cups all-purpose flour, plus extra for dusting

1 heaping teaspoon English mustard

1 tablespoon tomato paste

2 tablespoons balsamic or red wine vinegar

1 beef bouillon cube

3 ½ oz unsalted butter

1 big pinch of cayenne pepper

3 ½ oz full-fat cream cheese

1 large egg

Place a large saucepan on a medium-high heat, then put in the beef and a lug of oil. Fry for around 15 minutes, or until all the liquid has evaporated, breaking it down with a wooden spoon as you go. Peel and roughly chop the onions and add to the pan, strip in the thyme leaves, and cook for a further 10 minutes, or until the onions are soft and starting to brown. Stir in 1 heaping tablespoon of flour, followed by the mustard, tomato paste and vinegar. Crumble in the bouillon cube, pour in 2 ½ cups of boiling water, then simmer for 30 minutes, or until thickened, stirring occasionally. Season to perfection.

Meanwhile, put 1 ⅓ cups of flour, the butter, cayenne pepper and cream cheese into a food processor and pulse until it starts to come together. Tip out onto a flour-dusted work surface and pat and bring it together – try not to overwork it, or you'll have chewy, instead of lovely, crumbly pastry. Wrap in plastic wrap and leave to rest in the fridge until needed.

Preheat the oven to 350°F. Once the pie filling is ready, tip into a pie dish (roughly 10 inches). On a flour-dusted work surface, roll out the pastry so it's slightly bigger than your dish. Beat the egg, then brush the edge of the dish. Roll the pastry around your rolling pin, then unroll on top of the pie. Roughly trim away the excess, and pinch the edges to seal (use any leftover pastry to decorate the top, if you like). Brush the pastry with eggwash and bake for around 30 minutes on the middle shelf of the oven (45 minutes if cooking from cold), or until beautifully golden. Serve with seasonal veg.

MEATBALLS ALLA NORMA

Polenta in Italy is like mashed potatoes in Britain. Done properly and laced with Parmesan, it works really well with this spicy, sweet, beautifully cooked, Sicilian-inspired eggplant Norma sauce and the crispy, tasty meatballs. This is fun to cook and wonderful stodgy comfort food – I hope it becomes part of your repertoire.

Serves 4
Total time: 1 hour

559 calories

1 large eggplant

½ bunch of fresh Italian parsley (½ oz)

14 oz ground beef

1 tablespoon fennel seeds

olive oil

1 clove garlic

2 tablespoons sweet chili sauce

2 tablespoons balsamic vinegar

1 x 14-oz can of diced tomatoes

7 oz quick-cooking polenta

1 knob of unsalted butter

1 oz Parmesan cheese

Dice the eggplant into ½-inch cubes, then season well with salt and leave for 15 minutes. Meanwhile, finely chop the parsley (stalks and all), reserving a few leaves for garnish, and put into a bowl with the beef. Scrunch and mix together by hand, then divide into 20 equal pieces and roll into balls. Scatter the fennel seeds on a plate and roll the meatballs in them so they stick nicely, then pop into the fridge to firm up until needed.

Take handfuls of the eggplant and squeeze out the excess salty liquid, then put into a saucepan on a medium heat with a lug of oil to cook for 10 minutes, or until golden, stirring occasionally. Squash in the garlic through a garlic press, stir in the sweet chili sauce and balsamic, then tip in the tomatoes and a splash of water. Simmer for around 10 minutes, or until thickened.

Meanwhile, brown the meatballs in a separate saucepan on a medium heat with a lug of oil for about 10 minutes, or until golden all over and cooked through. Cook the polenta according to package instructions until you've got a good oozy consistency, adding the butter and a grating of Parmesan at the end. Season the sauce to perfection, then toss the meatballs through it and serve on top of the polenta, with the reserved parsley leaves scattered over and an extra grating of Parmesan, if you like.

CHINESE BEEF & TOFU

This is the most fantastic way of using tofu alongside beef — both of which are wonderful forms of protein — to create a delicious, comforting Chinese gravy-cum-sauce similar in texture to a Bolognese. Served with rice, a drizzle of chili sauce and a few friendly frozen peas for dabs of sweetness, this is a proper frugal favorite.

Serves 6
Total time: 50 minutes

465 calories

olive oil

7 oz ground beef

1 teaspoon Chinese five-spice powder

3 cloves garlic

1 thumb-sized piece of gingerroot

1 beef bouillon cube

1 heaping tablespoon cornstarch

⅔ cup black bean sauce

hot chili sauce

reduced-sodium soy sauce

17 oz basmati rice

12 oz silken tofu

1 ½ cups frozen peas

2 scallions

1 fresh red chile

optional: 4 sprigs of fresh cilantro

1 lime

Put a splash of oil, the beef, five-spice and a pinch of salt and pepper into a large saucepan on a medium heat and fry for around 15 minutes, or until all the liquid has evaporated, stirring occasionally. Meanwhile, peel and finely chop the garlic and ginger, then add them to the pan to fry for a further minute. Crumble in the bouillon cube, then stir in the cornstarch, followed by the black bean sauce and 1 tablespoon each of chili sauce and soy sauce. Pour in 2 cups of water, bring to a boil, then simmer for around 30 minutes, or until thickened and reduced, stirring occasionally.

With 15 minutes to go, cook the rice according to package instructions with a pinch of salt. When the sauce has thickened up really nicely, chop the tofu into ¾-inch cubes, place in a saucepan of simmering water with the frozen peas for 4 minutes, then carefully drain in a sieve. Gently stir the tofu and peas through the sauce, then season to perfection with a little soy sauce.

Trim and finely slice the scallions and chile, pick the cilantro leaves (if using), then sprinkle over the sauce. Serve with the fluffy rice and lime wedges for squeezing over, plus extra chili sauce for a real kick, if you like.

SNAKE IN THE HOLE

This dish is a bit of fun — it's the kind of recipe that makes the kids laugh, and ultimately we're all big kids at heart. Don't be mistaken by appearances, it's super delicious and I know you guys are going to make it and love it. It's a cross between a roasted meatloaf and a meatball, surrounded by our favorite Yorkshire pudding that cooks up around it and, if that's not enough, it's finished with a kiss of sweet onion gravy.

Serves 4 to 6

Total time: 1 hour

563 calories

¾ cup all-purpose flour

2 large eggs

⅓ cup reduced-fat (2%) milk

4 sprigs of fresh rosemary

2 slices of stale bread

1 lb ground beef

1 heaping teaspoon grainy mustard

1 sweet potato

olive oil

2 red onions

1 beef bouillon cube

balsamic vinegar

Preheat the oven to 400°F. Put ⅔ cup of flour into a pitcher with a pinch of salt, whisk in the eggs, then gradually add the milk until you have a smooth batter, and put aside. Pick the rosemary leaves and put half into a food processor, then blitz with the bread to make bread crumbs. Add the beef, a pinch of salt and pepper, and the mustard. Peel and coarsely grate in the sweet potato (this will keep the meatloaf really juicy) and pulse until combined. Shape into a snake about 1 ½ inches thick (be as realistic as you like), drizzle with a lug of oil and rub it all over. Place in an extra-large oiled roasting pan (roughly 12 x 14 inches). Roast for 20 minutes.

Meanwhile, to make the gravy, peel and slice the onions and put them into a saucepan on a medium heat with a lug of oil. Cook for about 15 minutes, or until softened, stirring regularly. Once soft, stir in the remaining flour, crumble in the bouillon cube and pour in 2 cups of water. Bring to a boil, then simmer for 20 minutes, or until you're happy with the consistency. Season to perfection, add a splash of balsamic, to taste, and keep warm.

When the time's up on the oven, slide out the snake pan, scatter in the remaining rosemary leaves and quickly and carefully pour in the batter. Return to the oven for around 25 minutes, or until the Yorkshire is golden and puffed up — don't be tempted to open the oven while it's cooking. Serve the pan in the middle of the table, pour the gravy around the snake and serve with a pot of mustard and steamed seasonal greens or a big bowl of peas (my kids always tuck into peas without fail) on the side.

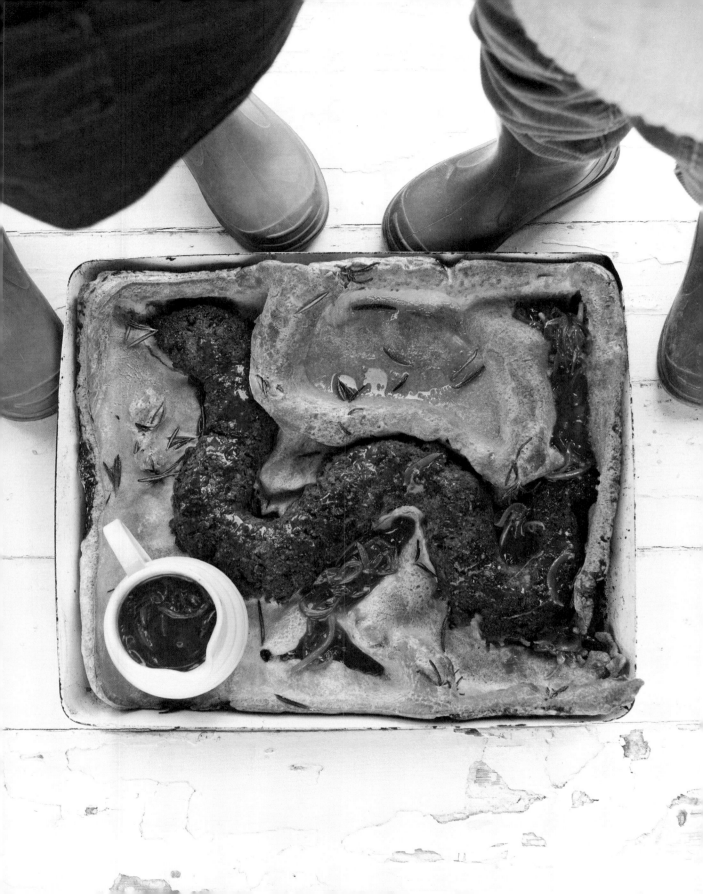

GO FIND THE . . .
SECRET STEAKS

Above and beyond the much-loved fillet, sirloin, rib-eye and rump there's an exciting world of incredible-value steaks, which I feel deliver amazing flavor and tenderness. The reality is, all animals are a patchwork quilt of muscles – tough ones that require slow cooking and tender ones you can cook quickly. So let me introduce you to four very underrated, unbelievably delicious steaks. Yes, these cuts are great value – they're often three times cheaper than a fillet – but they definitely have more flavor and can be nearly as tender. Here are my tips on how to cook them to achieve great results:

Cook them medium-rare to medium: Any more and they can tighten up, but to be honest, so can any steak.

Get the steak out of the fridge an hour before you cook it: Cooking from cold means that the heat doesn't get through to the core as efficiently and the juices don't react the same way either, so cook from room temperature.

Marinate for better flavor: A lug of olive oil, a swig of good vinegar and a nice woody herb (rosemary is a good one) rubbed into the steak is always going to help.

Season well, just before cooking: This is really important – sprinkle the steak with a good pinch of sea salt and freshly ground pepper when you're ready to cook.

Cook in a hot pan, grill pan or on a barbecue: For quality caramelization, essential for a delicious crust (also called bark).

Turn every minute until cooked to your liking: For really even internal cooking and to heighten the retention of juices.

Always rest for two minutes: Rub the steak with a little extra virgin olive oil or butter as it rests. Serve and carve in the middle of the table with a nice sharp carving knife, then pour over the resting juices – it looks great done like this, gets people excited, and you'll get more portions out of it.

WHAT TO ASK YOUR BUTCHER FOR:

Artisanal butcher Jack O'Shea gave me the correct wording so you can ask your butcher to find exactly the right cut for you. They're known by different names in North America, the UK and France, so I've given you as many names as I can.

1. BAVETTE, FLANK OR SKIRT:

This is a long, flat, delicious steak from the belly/abdomen, called skirt because it looks like a pleated skirt when you hold it up – this is the grain. I love cooking it whole – make sure you slice it against the grain, which is obvious to see.

2. HANGER, THICK SKIRT STEAK OR ONGLET:

This is a really interesting cut that sits as a muscle alongside the heart and organs. It therefore has a slightly stronger flavor – it's delicious, it's a nice-sized piece of meat and, with marinating and good cooking, it's a joy.

3. FLAT IRON STEAK OR FEATHER STEAK:

This is my favorite steak cut of the whole animal – I prefer it to any of the conventional cuts. It has beautiful flavor, texture and fat marbling, and is a good size. It's a steak that the butcher has to seam out of the shoulderblade in the forequarter of beef. There's a really tough sinew right in the middle of it, which once removed leaves you with the heavenly feather steak – ask your butcher to do this for you.

4. THIN SKIRT STEAK:

This skirt comes from around the rib cage and diaphragm. It's the least good-looking raw cut of meat, but once marinated is beautiful, and when quickly cooked on a screaming hot grill pan or barbecue, dressed with oil and a squeeze of lemon juice, and finely sliced, it really is a fantastic cut – try it.

SECRET STEAK & CHIPS
GARLICKY GREEN BEANS

This is a classic way to embrace any of those fantastic secret cuts of steak. For great results, cook your chosen steak hard and fast in a hot pan and preferably medium-rare, or possibly medium, but any more than that and it'll tighten and become chewy. With homemade wedge chips, garlicky green beans and a creamy mushroom sauce on the side, you know this has got Saturday night written all over it.

Serves 4

Total time: 50 minutes

1 ¾ lbs baking potatoes

olive oil

optional: 2 sprigs of fresh rosemary

1 small onion

3 ½ oz button mushrooms

3 tablespoons heavy cream

½ teaspoon Dijon mustard

14 oz frozen green beans

4 cloves garlic

1 x 1-lb flank, skirt or any of the other secret steaks (see page 148)

optional: 2 sprigs of fresh thyme or rosemary

Preheat the oven to 400°F. Scrub the potatoes, then halve and slice into wedges. Parboil in a large saucepan of boiling salted water for 4 minutes, then drain and tip into a roasting pan. Drizzle over a little oil, add a pinch of salt and pepper, then toss together, pick in the rosemary leaves (if using), and cook for 40 minutes, or until golden and crispy, shaking occasionally.

Meanwhile, peel the onion, then slice with the mushrooms and put into a medium saucepan on a medium heat with a drizzle of oil and a pinch of salt and pepper. Cook for 10 minutes, or until lightly golden, then add the cream, mustard and a splash of water and leave to simmer on a low heat, adding a splash more water, if needed, to stop it getting too thick. Put the frozen beans into a large frying pan on a medium heat with a lug of oil, stirring occasionally while they defrost. Peel and slice the garlic and add to the pan once all the liquid has evaporated from the beans, then turn the heat down and cook for about 5 minutes, or until crispy and golden.

Season the steak with salt and pepper and rub with a little oil, then pound with your fists to flatten and tenderize. Sear it in a large hot frying pan (cut the steak in half if you need to) on a high heat. Turn every minute for 5 to 6 minutes for medium-rare, or until cooked to your liking, and chuck in a couple of sprigs of fresh thyme or rosemary for the last 2 minutes, if you've got it. Remove to a board to rest for 2 minutes, then add any resting juices to the mushroom sauce and season it to perfection. Slice the steak thinly across the length (you'll notice there's a grain to the meat and you want to cut across that) and serve on top of the beans. Spoon over the mushroom sauce, and serve with the crispy wedges on the side.

SEARED BRITISH BEEF CARPACCIO

Lots of people absolutely love carpaccio, aka thin slivers of sweet-tasting raw meat, first made at Harry's Bar in Venice for an unwell customer who wasn't allowed to eat cooked meat (raw meat is easier to digest). So I've taken inspiration from the original and just sung a little bit of "Rule Britannia" into it with English mustard dressing, watercress and chunky orchard apple, all finished with shavings of good Cheddar cheese. Beautiful.

Serves 4

Total time: 25 minutes

1 x 10-oz bavette steak (see page 148)

olive oil

1 heaping teaspoon English mustard

1 tablespoon Worcestershire sauce

2 tablespoons cider vinegar

2 tablespoons extra virgin olive oil

3 ½ oz radishes

1 apple

3 ½ oz watercress

1 oz sharp Cheddar cheese

Put a grill pan or large frying pan on a high heat to get screaming hot. Rub the steak all over with salt, pepper and a drizzle of olive oil, then sear for 30 seconds on each side (you don't want to cook it – you're just lightly searing the outside). Remove to a board to rest for 5 minutes, then slice lengthways, just under ½ inch thick. Lay the slices, one by one, between two layers of plastic wrap and bash with a rolling pin or something heavy and flat until really thin. Arrange the slices beautifully over a large platter or divide them between individual plates as you go.

In a small bowl, whisk the mustard, Worcestershire sauce, vinegar and extra virgin olive oil together with a pinch of salt and pepper. Quarter or slice the radishes and cut the apple into wedges. Toss them with the watercress and a little of the dressing, then scatter over the steak. Drizzle over the rest of the dressing, then shave over the Cheddar using a vegetable peeler and serve in the middle of the table.

If you fancy a change, try swapping out apple for pear, watercress for arugula or pea shoots, and Cheddar for a nice bit of Lincolnshire Poacher or crumbly Lancashire cheese.

• PORK RECIPES •

Pork is a fantastic meat to buy, but in the spirit of *Save*, going for the more peripheral and unusual cuts like smoked hocks, belly and shoulder, and using ground meat, will help your wallet and offer brilliant flavor, if cooked correctly. This chapter is anchored in a beautiful roast shoulder recipe, plus a bundle of knockout leftover ideas that will definitely put a smile on your face. All the other recipes cover great-value cuts, so give them a go. My minimum standard when it comes to buying pork is Certified Humane. This meat will deliver great value, flavor and texture, and as with their chicken, this is farmed pork I would feel happy serving to my family. Please trade up to pasture-raised or organic meat wherever you can. Remember, buying a smaller amount of great-quality meat is a better investment.

MOTHERSHIP SUNDAY ROAST PORK

Pork shoulder is a cheaper cut, so it's great value, you always get fantastic flavor in your gravy from the dripping, you get the double bonus of cracklins – which we fight over in my house – and it's very forgiving during the cooking process. Make full use of the oven, cook a massive joint like this, and embrace the leftovers (see tip below left).

Serves 8 plus leftovers

Total time: 5 to 6 hours

417 calories

1 x 10-lb half shoulder of pork, bone in, skin on (ask your butcher to leave the skin on for you)

1 heaping tablespoon fennel seeds

olive oil

3 onions

10 fresh bay leaves

4 apples

2 red onions

1 head of red cabbage

2 tablespoons white wine vinegar

1 tablespoon berry jam

1 large celery root

1 heaping tablespoon all-purpose flour

> You'll get loads of leftover meat from a joint this size, so use some for amazing meals in the 2 to 3 days that follow, then portion up and freeze the rest for making meals in future weeks. Defrost in the fridge for 24 hours before cooking.

Preheat the oven to 425°F. Score the pork all over with a clean utility knife at ½-inch intervals and place in a large roasting pan (I've gone for the hand-end of the shoulder, but use the other half, if you prefer). Crush the fennel seeds in a pestle and mortar with a good pinch of salt and pepper. Rub all over the pork with a lug of oil, getting into the scores. Roast for 1 ½ hours. Meanwhile, peel and quarter the onions. When the time's up, pour away all the fat (save as dripping – see page 158), reduce the temperature to 250°F, and pop the onions and bay leaves underneath the pork in the pan. Pour in 3 cups of water, then cook for about 4 hours, or until the meat is juicy and easily pulls away from the bone. Halfway through, baste with the pan juices, then score around the diameter of the apples and add them to the pan with a splash of water, if needed.

With 40 minutes to go, peel and finely slice the red onions and put into a large saucepan on a medium heat with a lug of oil. Cook for 10 minutes, or until softened, stirring occasionally. Finely slice the cabbage in a food processor or by hand, and stir it into the pan with the vinegar, jam and a splash of water. Cook with the lid ajar for 20 to 25 minutes, or until tender, stirring occasionally, then season to perfection. Peel the celery root, cut into ¾-inch dice, then stir and fry in a saucepan on a high heat with a lug of oil and a pinch of salt for 10 to 15 minutes, or until golden. Reduce the heat to medium-low and cook with the lid ajar for around 15 minutes, stirring occasionally.

Remove the pork from the oven, transfer to a platter with the apples and cover. Put the pan (onions and all) on a medium heat on the stove and stir in the flour. You should have plenty of liquid to make your gravy, but top it up slightly with water, if needed, and add any pork resting juices. Stir well and simmer for 5 minutes, or until you're happy with the consistency. Pour and push the gravy through a sieve into a pitcher. Serve everything in the middle of the table, with seasonal greens, plus all your usual trimmings.

HAVE YOU EVER ...
THROWN AWAY THE DRIPPING FROM A ROAST DINNER?

First and foremost, dripping holds an incredible amount of flavor. If you start any stew, soup, ragù or simple tomato sauce with a tiny teaspoon of dripping, it's like using the best bouillon cube you could possibly have. Even fish, shellfish and vegetables will massively benefit from a little dripping in the cooking process, not to mention flatbreads and making the best roast potatoes (trust me, it'll make those delicious roasties even better). Yes, it's a saturated fat, but the whole point is you only use a little once in a while, and it sits in the fridge waiting to be used. It's stable, lasts for a couple of months, and used sparingly it's a wonderful weapon in tasty cooking.

Without question, our grandparents and their parents would have been incredibly passionate about using any leftover fat cooked out from beef, lamb, pork and chicken. They'd have called it "dripping," and I guess in this day and age, a lot of people will be worried about the amount of saturated fat they're consuming. It's correct that you're largely better off using fats lower in saturates, but, and this is a big but, if you're cooking fresh food as opposed to buying fast food and takeout, using a little dripping in your cooking in conjunction with fresh ingredients will undoubtedly give you less saturated fats than many processed foods. To me, it's the same as things like cream or cheese: we all love them, but they must definitely be used in moderation.

Throwing away fat is also really bad for the drainage system, and not good for the environment either, so use it up in cooking – just a little at a time – rather than discarding it.

Your simplest option is to pour the dripping into a clean jam jar – make sure it's not too hot, though, or it'll crack the glass – and store it in the fridge. I keep different drippings separate – beef, chicken, pork, duck, goose – but I don't tend to keep lamb dripping that often because the flavor is a little too strong for it to be used in a lot of cooking.

The other thing that's really nice to do is to get some random fresh woody herbs like sage, rosemary, bay and thyme, even fragrant spices like cloves, star anise, cardamom and fennel seeds – whatever you've got, really – and divide them between the little compartments of an ice-cube tray. Crushed garlic, grated ginger and sliced chile will also work really well like this. Carefully pour in the fat plus any Marmitey pan juices that come with it. Whack it into the freezer and those little flavor bombs will be sitting there waiting for you whenever you need them to start off your cooking with a bang.

AMERICAN HOT PIZZA PIE

LEFTOVER...

Blend the most widely eaten pizza in the UK, the American Hot, with the classic Chicago pizza pie (which was cooked in the pan because coal, the local fuel in Chicago, was turning the pizza bases black), and something magical happens. Served in this way, with leftover spiced pork and a kick from the chiles, the flavors are off the chart.

Serves 8 to 10

Total time: 1 hour
(plus proofing time)

644 calories

2 ¼ lbs strong white bread flour or Tipo "00" flour, plus extra for dusting

1 x ¼-oz sachet of active dry yeast

3 tablespoons extra virgin olive oil or leftover pork dripping

2 cloves garlic

1 teaspoon dried oregano

1 x 14-oz can of diced tomatoes

red wine vinegar

2 oz ciabatta or stale bread

olive oil

12 oz leftover cooked pork and cracklins or 6–8 good-quality lean pork sausages (preferably higher-welfare)

1 red onion

25 slices of pickled jalapeño or 2 fresh green chiles

5 oz Cheddar cheese or mozzarella

1 heaping teaspoon fennel seeds

1 good pinch of smoked paprika

Put the flour and 1 heaping teaspoon of sea salt into a large bowl and make a well in the middle. Add 2 ⅓ cups of tepid water to the well and stir in the yeast. Add the extra virgin olive oil (or the equivalent amount of leftover pork dripping, for incredible flavor), and use a fork to gradually bring in the flour, then pat together into a dough. Knead on a flour-dusted surface until smooth and springy. Place in a bowl, cover with a damp kitchen towel and leave somewhere warm until doubled in size (roughly 1 hour).

Meanwhile, peel and finely slice the garlic and put it into a blender with the oregano, tomatoes and 1 tablespoon of vinegar or liquid from the jalapeño jar. Whiz until smooth, season and put aside. In a food processor, blitz the bread into fine bread crumbs. Oil four round pans, roughly 12 inches wide (you can use ovenproof frying pans if you're cooking all the pizzas straight away), and lightly dust with the bread crumbs.

Preheat the oven to 375°F. Knock the dough back, then divide into four and stretch or roll out each piece on a flour-dusted surface to about 12 inches wide. Place in the pans, pushing the dough up the sides to create a crust, then let them proof for another 15 to 20 minutes. Divide the sauce between your pizza bases. Finely chop the pork and any leftover cracklins, or squeeze the meat out of the sausage skins, then sprinkle over the pizzas. Peel and finely slice the onion, toss it in a drizzle of olive oil and scatter over the top with the sliced jalapeños or chiles and bombs of cheese. Bash the fennel seeds and paprika in a pestle and mortar until fairly fine, then sprinkle over the pizzas from a height. At this point, I like to cover two pizzas with plastic wrap and pop them in the freezer for another day. Bake the remaining pizzas for around 15 to 20 minutes, or until the cheese has melted and the base is golden, puffed up and crispy. Delicious. You can cook your other pizzas straight from the freezer, just increase the time to 30 minutes and make sure they're piping hot throughout before serving.

BANH MI

Over recent decades, the Vietnamese community within London has grown, and with it of course has come some pretty special food. In street food markets all across the city, banh mi stands are pleasing locals with this flexible French-Vietnamese classic. Baguette, pâté, barbecued meat, pickles and chile – you can't go wrong.

Serves 4

Total time: 45 minutes

473 calories

1 carrot

¼ English cucumber

¼ head of white cabbage

1 tablespoon superfine sugar

3 tablespoons white wine vinegar

7 oz chicken livers

2 onions

½ bunch of fresh cilantro (½ oz)

olive oil

7 oz leftover cooked pork

optional: leftover pork dripping

2 tablespoons sweet chili sauce

1 fresh red chile

4 small French baguettes or subs

optional: hot chili sauce

Cut the carrot and cucumber into skinny matchsticks, shred the cabbage, then place all these in a bowl. Add the sugar, vinegar and a really good pinch of salt, and scrunch together for a minute to make a pickle. Put aside.

Trim the chicken livers, then soak in a bowl of water for a few minutes. Peel and finely chop the onions with the cilantro stalks and put into a large saucepan on a medium heat with a lug of oil. Cook for 10 minutes, or until softened, stirring regularly. Drain then chop the livers and add to the pan for a further 5 minutes, then tip it all into a food processor and blitz into a semi-smooth pâté. Scrape into a bowl and season to perfection.

Wipe out the pan and return it to a medium heat, then slice up the pork and add with a spoonful of leftover dripping, if you've got it, or a drizzle of oil. Fry for 5 minutes, or until crispy and hot through, tossing with the sweet chili sauce for the last minute. Finely slice the chile.

Halve the baguettes lengthways (warm them through in a hot oven for 10 minutes first, if you can) and generously spread both sides with the pâté. Squeeze out and discard the excess salty liquid from the pickled veg and pile into the baguettes. Top with crispy pork, fresh chile and cilantro leaves, then drizzle with hot chili sauce, if you dare, and tuck in.

DIM SUM PORK BUNS

LEFTOVER...

It's always a lot of fun to make stuffed buns, and when you steam them and they grow and puff up, I find people get really excited. I've always enjoyed dim sum for Chinese brunch, but actually these are also really good for parties, with a beer. Steam in batches to keep them fresh and soft – everyone will go mad for them.

Serves 8

Total time: 45 minutes

323 calories

1 fresh red chile

4 scallions

½ bunch of fresh cilantro (½ oz)

10 oz leftover cooked pork

4 heaping tablespoons black bean sauce

2 tablespoons hot chili sauce

3 ¾ cups self-rising flour, plus extra for dusting

1 ⅔ cups reduced-fat (2%) milk

2 tablespoons raw sesame seeds

1 head of bibb lettuce

hoisin sauce, to serve

Seed the chile and trim and halve 2 scallions. Very finely slice them lengthways, put them into a little bowl of ice-cold water so they curl up, add the cilantro leaves, then put aside. Trim and finely chop the remaining scallions and place in a bowl. Pull the pork into fine shreds, add to the bowl along with the black bean and chili sauces, and mix well.

By hand or in a food processor, mix the flour and milk until combined. Add a sprinkling more flour, if needed, to bring it together, then tip onto a flour-dusted work surface and roll into a thick sausage. Cut into 16 pieces and roll into balls, then flatten each one into a round about ¼ inch thick. Place a heaping teaspoon of pork mixture in the center of each round, then fold and pull the edges up over the filling, pinching the ends together really well to seal. Place upside down, so the seam is at the bottom, in double-layered large cupcake paper liners in a steamer basket — you should get 8 in at a time, so you'll need to steam them in two batches, or you can simply do two layers at once, if you've got two baskets.

Put a wok on a medium heat and quickly toast the sesame seeds, then tip them into a small bowl, put aside, and add ¾ inch of boiling water to the wok (top up between batches, if needed). Add the steamer basket of buns, pop the lid on, cook for around 12 minutes, or until the buns are fluffy and hot in the middle, then sprinkle with a quarter of the sesame seeds. Serve the buns in the middle of the table with a stack of lettuce leaves, hoisin sauce and a bowl with most of the sesame seeds for dipping, and with the drained curly chile, scallions and cilantro leaves on the side for sprinkling over. Repeat with the second basket of buns, sprinkling with the remaining sesame seeds before serving.

SLOW-ROASTED PORK RAGÙ

LEFTOVER...

Leftover pork adds a phenomenal amount of flavor to this sauce, which would be impossible to achieve with ground meat. It's simple to make and is wonderful, as you can see here, served with any pasta or hot bruschetta – or, as we say in Britain, "toast." Really, the list of things you can serve it with is ridiculous: in sandwiches, with polenta or a jacket spud, in risotto, in cannelloni, even in tiramisù . . . joking, I was just checking you're still concentrating!

Serves 6
Total time: 50 minutes

2 sprigs of fresh rosemary

2 cloves garlic

2 onions

2 carrots

olive oil

½ teaspoon dried chili flakes

1 heaping teaspoon fennel seeds

10 oz leftover cooked pork

3 ¼ cups passata

Pick the rosemary leaves, peel the garlic, onion and carrots, then finely chop them all and put into a large saucepan on a medium heat with a lug of oil and the dried chili flakes. Crush the fennel seeds in a pestle and mortar, stir into the pan and fry for 15 minutes, or until soft and sticky, stirring regularly.

Meanwhile, cut the pork into ½-inch chunks. When the veg are soft, stir the pork into the pan and fry for 5 more minutes, then add the passata. Add a splash of water to the empty passata jar, swirl it around, then pour it into the pan. Simmer gently for around 20 minutes, or until the pork breaks up and the sauce is thickened and reduced, stirring occasionally and adding another splash or two of water, if needed. Season to perfection, then I like to serve it with freshly cooked pasta or toasted sourdough. Adding a grating of your favorite cheese will finish it off nicely.

Whenever you use passata, pop the empty jar through the dishwasher and reuse it to store homemade pickles (see page 176), chutneys or flavored oils and vinegars (see page 70).

CRISPY PORK TACOS

LEFTOVER…

I love a good taco. I've shown you how to make soft tacos in the fish chapter (see page 220), and they're amazing, but, going along with the crispy pork and cracklins vibe, I'm using crunchy tacos here. The contrast with tasty, stodgy black beans, salad and chiles is incredible. Find a quiet spot and eat messily, but very happily.

Serves 6

Total time: 30 minutes

395 calories

1 green bell pepper

1 large red onion

1 fresh green chile

1 pinch of ground cloves

2 tablespoons red wine vinegar

optional: leftover pork dripping

olive oil

2 tablespoons Cajun seasoning

2 x 14-oz cans of black beans

10 oz leftover cooked pork

leftover pork cracklins

1 level teaspoon sweet smoked paprika

12 taco shells

½ head of iceberg lettuce

6 tablespoons fat-free plain yogurt

Seed the pepper and peel the onion. Finely slice the pepper and half the onion, ideally in a food processor or on a mandolin (use the guard!), or by hand using good knife skills. Very finely slice the chile by hand, then tip all these into a bowl with the cloves, vinegar and a really good pinch of salt. Gently scrunch together to make a pickle and leave to one side.

Finely chop the remaining onion half and put it into a medium saucepan on a medium-low heat, ideally with a spoonful of leftover pork dripping from the mothership roast (if you have it), or a lug of oil, and the Cajun seasoning. Fry for 8 to 10 minutes, or until sweet and lightly golden, stirring occasionally, then tip in the beans (juice and all). Bring to a boil, mash slightly, then season to perfection and leave on a low heat to simmer gently and thicken for a few minutes, but don't let them dry out.

Meanwhile, cut the pork and any leftover cracklins into ½-inch dice and put into a medium frying pan on a medium heat with a splash of oil. Sprinkle with the paprika and fry for 5 to 8 minutes, or until dark and gnarly. Warm the tacos according to package instructions, and shred the lettuce.

When you're ready to go, load up the tacos with shredded lettuce, stodgy beans and the crispy pork and cracklins. Squeeze the onion and pepper pickle to get rid of the excess salty liquid, then add a little handful to each taco, top with a dollop of yogurt and tuck in.

BBQ PULLED PORK
WAFFLES & SLAW

LEFTOVER...

Soft and crunchy waffles, tender BBQ pork and zingy slaw – what a combo. It's delicious, moreish food and brilliant for using up leftover pork from either the piri piri pork belly (see page 182) or the mothership Sunday roast pork (see page 156). I have to be honest, a waffle iron makes all the difference here, but you can get them fairly cheaply online. If you don't have one, use a grill pan, cooking two "waffles" at a time, instead.

Serves 4

Total time: 40 minutes

442 calories

½ red onion

1 carrot

¼ head of white cabbage

½ bunch of fresh mint (½ oz)

1 fresh red chile

2 tablespoons white wine vinegar

2 tablespoons extra virgin olive oil

1 ½ tablespoons unsalted butter

1 large egg

1 tablespoon superfine sugar

1 cup self-rising flour

½ teaspoon baking soda

¾ cup reduced-fat (2%) milk

10 oz leftover cooked pork

4 heaping tablespoons BBQ sauce

optional: leftover pork cracklins

Peel the onion and carrot, trim the cabbage, then coarsely grate them on a box grater or in a food processor. Pick the mint leaves and finely slice them with the chile, then scrunch all these together with the vinegar and oil to make a punchy slaw. Season to perfection and put aside.

Melt the butter in a small frying pan. Separate the egg into two bowls, making sure the white is in a squeaky-clean bowl. Whisk the white with the sugar until it forms stiff peaks. Whisk the yolk with the melted butter (put the pan aside for later), the flour and baking soda, then gradually whisk in the milk until you have a really smooth batter. Fold in the egg white mixture with a metal spoon. Get your waffle iron hot and ready to go, then cook according to instructions, until golden, light and fluffy.

Meanwhile, pull apart the leftover pork with two forks, mix with the BBQ sauce and put into the small frying pan on a medium heat to get nice and hot. Snap up any leftover cracklins and add that too, if you have it. Pile the hot pulled pork and slaw on top of your waffles, and tuck in!

Any type of leftover meat will be brilliant served in this way – as long as you can tear it apart, you're on to a winner.

PULLED PORK PEPPERS
EASY BAKED RISOTTO

LEFTOVER...

This is one of those fabulous, comforting dinners that really takes very little time to put together, and uses leftover pork to great effect. You just whack it all into the oven and let time work its magic. This is a really good method for a baked risotto, and very low maintenance, and the two dishes eat ridiculously well together.

Serves 4

Total time: 1 hour

613 calories

2 large mixed-color bell peppers

olive oil

1 onion

2 ripe tomatoes

½ bunch of fresh Italian parsley (½ oz)

2 tablespoons red wine vinegar

1 tablespoon tomato ketchup

1 heaping teaspoon sweet smoked paprika

7 oz leftover cooked pork

10 oz risotto or Arborio rice

1 vegetable bouillon cube

1 knob of unsalted butter

2 oz Parmesan cheese

1 lemon

Preheat the oven to 350°F. Halve and seed the peppers, rub them with oil, salt and pepper, then place them in a snug-fitting baking dish, cut-side up. Peel and finely slice a quarter of the onion and put to one side, then finely chop the rest, put into a medium ovenproof dish and mix with 2 lugs of oil. Place both dishes in the oven for 20 minutes. Meanwhile, coarsely grate or finely chop the tomatoes and finely chop the parsley stalks. Put them into a bowl with the vinegar, ketchup, paprika, reserved sliced onion and a lug of oil. Shred or chop the pork, add it to the bowl and scrunch everything together until really well mixed.

Take the two dishes out of the oven. To the onion dish, add the rice and a pinch of salt and pepper, then crumble in the bouillon cube, pour in 4 cups of boiling water, stir and carefully return it to the oven. Working fairly quickly, pour any liquid from the peppers into the pork mixture, stir together, then divide evenly between the peppers and return the dish to the oven too. Cook everything for 26 minutes, or until the peppers are golden, the risotto is oozy and the rice is cooked through but still holds its shape, stirring the rice occasionally. Stir the butter and finely grated Parmesan through the risotto at the end, season to perfection, if needed, and finish with a good grating of lemon zest. Roughly chop the parsley leaves, scatter them over the peppers, and serve everything right away.

JERKED BBQ RIBS

Let's be honest for a minute — there's nothing better than tearing the sweet meat off a gnarly, sticky rib. Ribs should always be nice and economical to get hold of, and whenever I've told people that's what's for dinner, they've always looked really happy. This method is so simple, but the end result is phenomenally tasty.

Serves 6

Total time: 2 hours 25 minutes
(plus marinating)

782 calories

1 onion

6 cloves garlic

1–2 Scotch bonnet chiles

3 fresh bay leaves

1 x 8-oz can of pineapple chunks in juice

1 ½ tablespoons ground cumin

½ tablespoon hot chili powder

1 tablespoon ground allspice

2 tablespoons dried thyme

2 tablespoons white wine vinegar

2 tablespoons Worcestershire sauce

2 tablespoons English mustard

¾ cup tomato ketchup

½ cup brown sugar

12 meaty side ribs (5 ½–6 ½ lbs)

Peel and quarter the onion, peel the garlic, seed the chiles and pull the stalks out of the bay leaves, then put all these into a blender with all of the remaining ingredients, except the ribs. Blitz everything until smooth and pour into a large bowl. Add the ribs, turning to make sure they're all well coated, then cover the bowl and leave to marinate in the fridge for at least 2 hours, but preferably overnight.

Preheat the oven to 275°F. Place the ribs in a couple of large roasting pans, leaving the sauce behind in the bowl. Cover with a double layer of aluminum foil, then roast for 2 hours. Meanwhile, pour the sauce into a saucepan, bring to a boil, then simmer on a medium-low heat for around 10 minutes, or until thickened. Taste the sauce – if you want to tweak the flavor and make it more spicy, do that now with a little extra chili powder.

When the time's up on the ribs, drain away the juices from the pan, pouring enough into the sauce to give you a brushable consistency (save the rest for making a delicious spicy gravy another day), then turn the oven up to 425°F. Generously brush the ribs with some of the sauce every 5 minutes, turning each time, for a further 20 minutes, or until shiny, sticky and gnarly. Serve with any remaining sauce drizzled on top. Great with the usual suspects – rice or potato wedges, and a big green salad – and a good sprinkle of your favorite pickle. My house pickle (see page 176) complements these tasty ribs a treat.

HAVE YOU EVER ...
THROWN AWAY RANDOM, LEFTOVER BITS OF VEG?

The fact is, a lot of people do, so next time you open the fridge and see leftover veg, instead of wasting these lonely fellas, why not partake in one of the coolest kitchen tricks by making your own great little house pickle? You get a good couple of months out of it, it's my favorite way to use up odds and ends of crunchy veg that would otherwise get chucked away, and it gives you a fantastic pickle that will work with all sorts of dishes.

Obviously I don't know how much leftover veg and what type you've got, but take anything firm and crunchy that pickles nicely, such as broccoli (including the stalk), carrots, radishes, celery, French beans, cucumber, any cabbages, snow peas, cauliflower, beets or onion (and the list goes on) – and simply cut or slice them up fine or chunky, depending on what you're looking for. I quite like purposely cutting each vegetable differently – some diced, some into erratic chunks, some sliced delicately and some more thickly. I've even got a crinkle-cut knife now and I'm loving it – you should get one! This variation in size and texture will give you a fabulous pickle, and all you need to do is cover it with the pickling liquid (see below). You might want to double or treble the quantities, depending on what you've got left over and how big your jar is – feel free to make it your own.

Put 1 mug of water and 2 mugs of your chosen vinegar (white wine, red wine, cider or malt) into an appropriately sized clean airtight jar with 1 heaping tablespoon each of sea salt and sugar, and stir until the sugar has dissolved. You can spike the liquid with any herbs or spices that you love – I've found mustard seeds, dill, chile and coriander all work well.

You could even get creative and have two jars on the go – one sweet and sour, and one hot and spicy. Add your veg to the jar and keep it in the fridge for up to 8 weeks. You can absolutely use it right away – it will start off quite sharp and crunchy, then relax into itself over a period of a few weeks.

These brilliant house pickles are fantastic in sandwiches and salads, lovely on a cheeseboard, and great beside curries and stir-fries. You can finely chop the veg to go in dressings or to be mixed into ketchup and dolloped on a burger, and the vinegary liquid can even be added to dressings as your acidic element, so you're getting double use and double pleasure.

If you're going round to someone's house for dinner, instead of a bottle of wine, why not give a cute jar of your homemade house pickle? Label it up and make it look extra special.

Watch out for red or purple veg like beets, radishes, red onions and red cabbage – they're delicious but tend to turn everything else in the jar pink, so I like to keep them in their own pink little world.

PORK MEATLOAF
SPAGHETTI SAUCE

Waiters and senior chefs used to love the meatloaf I cooked for staff lunches as a young chef. I'd use leftovers and trimmings of pork, beef and lamb, then roast the loaf and serve it with spaghetti and a spicy tomato sauce. I swear, taking pride in staff lunches on a really tight budget got me extra promotions in the kitchen. I've just used ground pork here, but feel free to use any blend of ground meat – lamb, beef and game all work well too.

Serves 6

Total time: 1 hour

3 carrots

olive oil

3 ½ oz stale bread

1 lb ground pork

2 heaping teaspoons dried oregano

1 oz feta cheese

1 large egg

3 fresh red chiles

1 onion

2 cloves garlic

3 ¼ cups passata

1 oz Cheddar cheese

17 oz dried spaghetti

The chiles add great depth to this sauce, but if your kids won't eat them, simply leave them out.

Preheat the oven to 400°F. Peel the carrots, quarter lengthways, then place in a roasting pan (roughly 10 x 12 inches), drizzle with oil and cook for 10 minutes. Meanwhile, blitz the bread into bread crumbs in a food processor, then use your hands to mix in a bowl with the pork, half the oregano, the crumbled feta (it's a small amount, but it makes all the difference!), the egg and a good pinch of salt and pepper. Shape into a loaf (roughly 8 inches long), then, when the time's up on the carrots, make a space in the middle of the pan and add the meatloaf. Cook for a further 25 minutes, or until the meatloaf is golden and cooked through.

Meanwhile, halve the chiles lengthways and seed, then put them into a medium saucepan on a low heat with a lug of oil for 2 minutes while you peel and finely chop the onion and garlic. Scoop out and reserve the chiles, then put the onion and garlic into the pan with the remaining oregano and fry for about 10 minutes, or until softened, stirring regularly. Pour in the passata, add a splash of water to the empty jar, swirl it around and pour into the pan, season to perfection, then simmer until the time's up on the meatloaf.

Remove the pan from the oven and carefully pour the sauce around the meatloaf. Pull the carrots to the top of the sauce and arrange around the meatloaf with the chiles, then grate the Cheddar on top of it (I like to sprinkle over a few fresh woody herb leaves like rosemary at this point, if I've got them). Pop the meatloaf back into the oven for a further 5 to 10 minutes, or until golden and delicious, and the sauce is bubbling. Meanwhile, cook the spaghetti in a large saucepan of boiling salted water according to package instructions, then drain. Serve everything in the middle of the table with a salad, then slice up the meatloaf, mashing the chiles into the sauce for added heat, if you like.

SAUSAGE PANZANELLA

Good stale bread is the hero here – torn up and toasted, it acts like a sponge and sucks up all the incredible flavor from the tomatoes and hot dressing. It's a get-out-of-jail-free recipe for using leftover bread, helping you to waste less, but if you don't have any, simply tear up a fresh loaf and bake it for slightly longer. If you shop smart, this recipe is also perfect for using the super-ripe, cheap tomatoes you can buy in bulk from markets at the end of the day.

Serves 4

Total time: 35 minutes

583 calories

7 oz quality stale bread

12 black olives, with pits

2 heaping teaspoons capers

2 lbs ripe mixed tomatoes

1 small red onion

1 bunch of fresh basil (1 oz)

½ clove of garlic

3 tablespoons red or white wine vinegar

5 tablespoons extra virgin olive oil

2 good-quality lean pork sausages
   (preferably higher-welfare)

2 level teaspoons sweet smoked paprika

1 heaping teaspoon fennel seeds

olive oil

2 sprigs of fresh rosemary

10 oz ripe cherry or grape tomatoes

1 ½ oz Parmesan cheese

Preheat the oven to 375°F. Tear the bread into thumb-sized pieces, place in a roasting pan, and pop into the oven for around 15 minutes, or until crisp and golden. Meanwhile, pit the olives and place in a small bowl with the capers and a splash of boiling water.

Roughly chop the 2 pounds of mixed tomatoes, peel the onion and slice as finely as you can, and pick the basil leaves (reserving the stalks and a handful of baby leaves). In a big bowl, toss the chopped tomatoes with the basil leaves and most of the onion, then put half the mixture into a blender with the basil stalks, peeled garlic, vinegar and extra virgin olive oil and blitz until smooth. Season, then pour the dressing back into the bowl, add the olives, capers and soaking water, and toss with the toasted bread – it will look like a lot of dressing, but don't worry, the bread will soak it all up.

Squeeze the meat out of the sausages into a cold frying pan and add the paprika and fennel seeds. Place on a medium heat with a splash of olive oil and fry until golden, breaking up the meat with a wooden spoon. When lightly golden, pick in the rosemary leaves and fry for just another minute.

Taste the salad and season to perfection, if needed, then transfer to a nice serving platter and pour the contents of the frying pan over the top. Halve or quarter the cherry or grape tomatoes and scatter over the salad with the reserved baby basil leaves and remaining finely sliced onion. Use a vegetable peeler to shave over the Parmesan, and serve.

PIRI PIRI PORK BELLY

A lot of people seem to be having a bit of a love affair with piri piri at the moment, and I thought I'd take this opportunity to roast one of my favorite cuts of pork in the sauce, so that the flavor from the pork is flavoring that sauce, and vice versa. Even better, the oven does most of the work for you – good times.

Serves 6

Total time: 2 hours 30 minutes

670 calories

6 fresh bay leaves

1 level teaspoon smoked paprika

1 tablespoon olive oil

2 ½ lbs pork belly, skin on, bone in

2 red onions

1 sweet potato

4 cloves garlic

2 fresh red chiles

1 tablespoon red wine vinegar

3 ¼ cups passata

2 sprigs of fresh rosemary

If you're feeding less than six people and have leftovers, they're fantastic used in the BBQ pulled pork recipe on page 170.

Preheat the oven to 400°F. Tear out the stalks from the bay leaves, then bash the leaves in a pestle and mortar with a good pinch of salt into a paste. Add the paprika and muddle in the oil. Score the pork all over in a criss-cross fashion with a clean utility knife at ½-inch intervals, just going through the fat, not the meat. Rub with the bay oil, getting into all the scores. Peel and roughly chop the onions and sweet potato, peel and finely chop the garlic and halve the chiles, then place it all in a snug-fitting roasting pan or dish and sit the pork on top. Roast for 45 minutes.

Take the pan out of the oven and remove the pork to a plate momentarily. Stir the vinegar and passata into the pan, half fill the empty passata jar with water, swirl it around and pour into the pan, then sit the pork back on top. Reduce the oven temperature to 325°F and roast for a further 1 ½ hours. Twenty minutes before the end, remove the pork from the oven and skim the fat from the surface into a small bowl. Strip in the rosemary leaves (discarding the stalks), toss to coat, then sprinkle over the pork belly and place back in the oven for the remaining time, or until the pork is golden and tender and the sauce is reduced (loosen with a splash of extra water at the end, if needed). The cracklins should have puffed up nicely, but if it hasn't (pork skin can sometimes be erratic), just pop it under a hot broiler and watch it like a hawk until it's perfect. Serve in the middle of the table with your chosen sides (see below), and tuck in.

This is great served with pretty much anything you'd expect to enjoy on the side – bread, a stack of toast, pita, freshly cooked spaghetti or rice, and a nice big salad, of course.

TOO MANY CHILES?

With all you fellow chile lovers out there, I'm sure you've often been in a position where you've bought a package of chiles and you only need one or two for a recipe, so you end up with a bunch left over. Don't let them shrivel up – let me show you how to use them, waste less and create some tasty flavor weapons for clever cooking.

FREEZE

Pop leftover chiles into the top drawer of your freezer in a bag or plastic container. They're fantastic finely grated directly from frozen, which creates a tasty, beautiful chile dust that is great in cooking and for marinating, or for sprinkling over pastas, salads, starters, antipasti, meat or fish dishes. Yum.

PICKLE

Slice up leftover chiles and pickle them. I particularly love using the leftover juice from jars of gherkins or dill pickles for this. Instead of throwing it away, I top up the jar with a little vinegar, stir in a couple of teaspoons of sea salt, and just throw in a load of sliced chiles. It holds them in a nice environment to be used in all sorts of dishes for a couple of months.

PLANT

Save seeds from dried chiles (see right) in an envelope over the winter and have a go at growing your own. Sow the seeds indoors in February or March (at about 70°F) to germinate, then grow them somewhere warm and light, such as a sunny windowsill or conservatory, potting them up as required. Feed them every 10 days – my gardener Pete uses a natural liquid seaweed fertilizer – and mist them regularly with water.

OIL

There are two types of oil you can make, using fresh or dried chiles. With fresh chiles, once you've got about 10 leftover chiles saved up in the freezer (or 10 on your plant!), place them in a snug-fitting pan and cover with ¾ inch of cheap olive oil. Pop on a low heat and slowly simmer them for 1 hour, then allow to cool. Next I like to remove and discard the stalks and seeds, scrape the chiles into a clean jam jar, pour over the infused oil and fill to the top with regular olive oil. This will give you a round, warm, sweet-tasting oil. Dried chili oil really couldn't be simpler. Crumble up a mixture of dried chiles (see below) – flaked or ground – then heat them in a dry pan for 1 minute, cover with cheap olive oil, put back into a bottle, and whenever you remember, just give it a shake to ensure maximum flavor infusion. This will give you a savory, simpler oil that can be used in lots of different ways.

DRY

Dry whole chiles in a warm place near a radiator, or in an airing cupboard or dehydrator or, if it's a really nice day, dry them in natural sunlight on a dark tray to maximize heat. Once dry, whack them whole into a jar, then crumble or flake them as needed in or over any of the dishes listed under Freeze.

SPICED SAUSAGE CASSOULET

In the spirit of super-tasty affordable food, I've spiced up a simple, rustic sausage cassoulet with the addition of a little pork belly. It's simple to put together, then just chugs away, becoming more and more intense in flavor as it cooks. It's made even more delicious served with toasted bread rubbed with tomato and garlic. Enjoy!

Serves 4

Total time: 1 hour 20 minutes

744 calories

5 oz pork belly, skin off, bone out

4 good-quality lean pork sausages
 (preferably higher-welfare)

olive oil

2 carrots

1 red onion

1 teaspoon sweet smoked paprika

3 ¼ cups passata

1 x 14-oz can of cannellini beans

½ bunch of fresh rosemary (½ oz)

1 ciabatta loaf

1 clove garlic

2 ripe cherry or grape tomatoes
 or 1 ripe tomato

extra virgin olive oil

This is a fantastic humble base recipe, but if you have access to other meat or game, a few chunks of things like rabbit, duck or pheasant added in here would also be delicious.

Preheat the oven to 350°F. Carefully cut the pork belly into 12 chunky lardons and put into a large ovenproof casserole pan on a medium heat with the sausages and a lug of olive oil. Keep them moving while you peel the carrots and slice into chunks at an angle, and peel the onion and cut into wedges. When the pork belly and sausages are lightly golden, remove the sausages and carefully slice each one into three at an angle, then put back into the pan with the carrots, onion and paprika and cook for a further 15 minutes, stirring regularly.

Tip the passata into the pan. Half fill the empty passata jar with water, swirl it around and pour into the pan. Drain and add the cannellini beans and a pinch of salt and pepper, then stir well. Cover with aluminum foil and place in the oven for 20 minutes. Meanwhile, pick and roughly chop the rosemary leaves, then toss them in a lug of olive oil. When the time's up on the cassoulet, remove and discard the foil, then sprinkle with the oiled rosemary and place back in the oven for a further 30 minutes, or until thick and delicious.

Meanwhile, halve the ciabatta lengthways and pop it into the oven when the cassoulet has roughly 20 minutes to go. Halve the garlic clove and rub it all over the ciabatta a couple of times during cooking to build up flavor. Remove the cassoulet pan and ciabatta from the oven, then halve the tomatoes and rub them all over the bread, drizzle it with extra virgin olive oil and sprinkle with a small pinch of salt. Serve right away next to the cassoulet, to soak up all that lovely sauce.

SMOKED HAM HOCKS
PARSLEY SAUCE

Smoked ham hocks can be picked up super cheaply and will feed three people, so they're fantastic value. They're also full of flavor, and the bone and smoke add loads of extra depth. This is gorgeous dinner-time comfort food and really good on colder days. Brilliant served with simply steamed greens on the side.

Serves 6 to 8

Total time: 3 hours
(plus soaking time)

2 x 1 ¾-lb smoked ham hocks, skin on

3 large onions

8 large carrots

2 ½ lbs potatoes

4 fresh bay leaves

4 sprigs of fresh thyme

2 bunches of fresh curly or
  Italian parsley (2 oz)

1 ½ tablespoons unsalted butter

2 tablespoons all-purpose flour

2 cups reduced-fat (2%) milk

2 teaspoons English mustard

1 tablespoon white wine vinegar

Place the ham hocks in a large, deep casserole pan, cover with cold water and place in the fridge overnight so the ham hocks can soak.

The next day, preheat the oven to 325°F. Drain the ham hocks and return them to the pan. Peel and roughly chop the onions and carrots, peel and halve the potatoes, and add to the pan with 3 bay leaves and the thyme. Just cover with cold water, put on a high heat and bring to a boil, then simmer for 20 minutes, skimming away any scum from the surface.

Place a piece of wet parchment paper roughly the same size and shape as the pan on top of the hocks, then transfer to the oven for 2 ½ hours, or until tender. Meanwhile, pick and roughly chop the parsley leaves and finely chop the stalks. Melt the butter in a saucepan on a medium heat, then stir in the flour to make a paste. Add the milk, a splash at a time, stirring continuously until you have a white sauce. Stir in the mustard, vinegar, the remaining bay leaf, all of the parsley stalks and most of the leaves, then season to perfection. Leave to bubble away gently for around 15 minutes, or until you have a drizzling consistency. Put to one side, and reheat when you need it.

When done, remove the ham hocks to a big platter. Arrange the veg around the edge, pour over the parsley sauce, scatter over the remaining parsley leaves and serve with seasonal greens. Take to the table and attack it, pushing the bones and skin to one side as you serve. Heaven.

Use any leftover broth to make a super-quick pea and ham soup – cook peeled, diced potatoes in the broth, adding frozen peas for the last couple of minutes, then blitz and stir in any leftover shreds of ham.

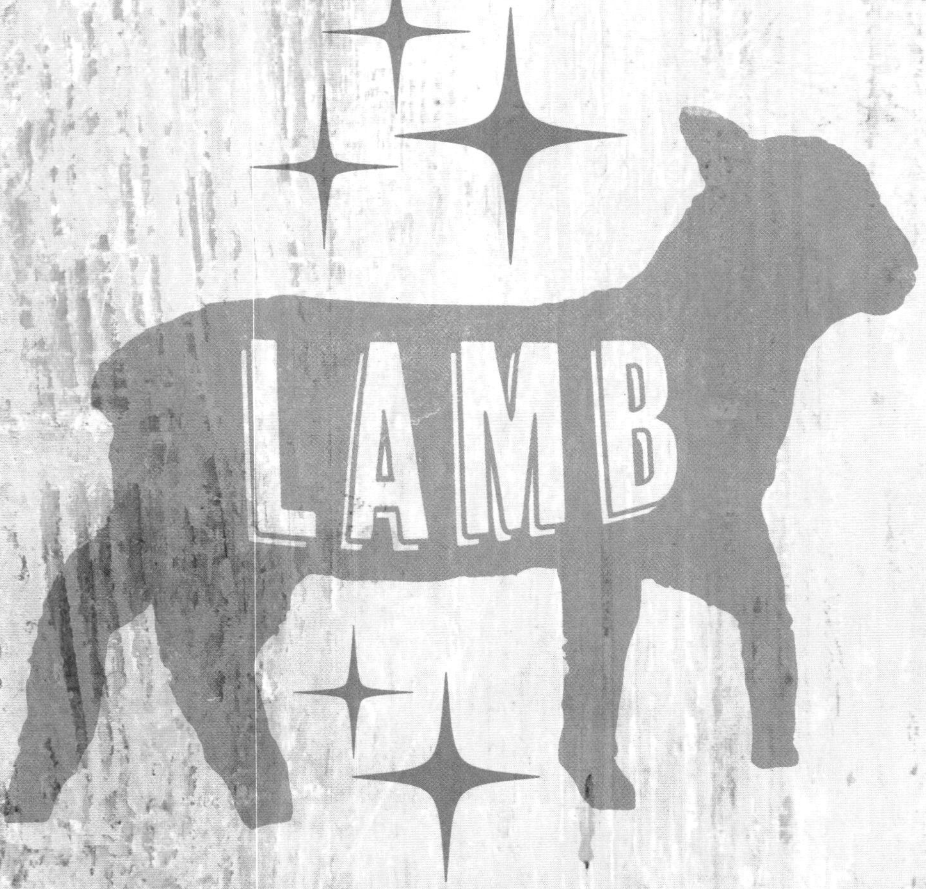
LAMB

• LAMB RECIPES •

North American lamb can be of excellent quality when raised by passionate artisan producers. It's important to look out for lamb that is grass-fed, pasture-raised or clearly labelled "Animal Welfare Approved" or "Certified Humane." To make sure you're getting quality meat, ask your butcher about the lamb's origins. In general, lamb's not cheap, but if you keep your eyes peeled, communicate with your butcher and use less pricey cuts like breast, neck, shoulder and offal, you'll get a great meal, and incredible flavor. Lamb sometimes gets a raw deal on the love front in comparison to the mighty beef, tasty pork and popular chicken, so I want to prove how fantastic it can be with a mega Sunday roast and an army of brilliant leftover dishes, all followed by a handful of amazing-value recipes that I'm sure you'll love.

MOTHERSHIP SUNDAY ROAST LAMB

Roast shoulder of lamb gives you the most tender, sweet, delicious meat that just falls off the bone – it's definitely my favorite cut of lamb for roasting. Cooked in this way, you can get everything you want for a good price, feed six people and have loads of leftovers. Keep the bones and any spare mint sauce for later recipes too.

Serves 6 plus leftovers

Total time: 4 hours 15 minutes

664 calories

1 head of garlic

1 bunch of fresh rosemary (1 oz)

olive oil

1 x 5 ½-lb shoulder of lamb, bone in

3 onions

3 lbs potatoes

1 bunch of fresh mint (1 oz)

1 teaspoon superfine sugar

3 tablespoons white wine vinegar

4 rashers of smoked bacon

1 large head of Savoy cabbage

1 tablespoon all-purpose flour

3 ¼ cups frozen peas

If you're not going to use all the leftover lamb within 2 or 3 days, simply portion it up and freeze for making meals in future weeks. Defrost in the fridge for 24 hours before cooking.

Preheat the oven to 325°F. In a pestle and mortar, bash 4 peeled garlic cloves, half the rosemary leaves and a pinch of salt and pepper into a paste, then muddle in a good lug of oil. Stab the lamb ten times, then stick your finger in each hole and massage the marinade in and all over. Peel and quarter the onions and place in a snug-fitting roasting pan (this is important), with the lamb on top. Add 3 tablespoons of water, cover tightly with aluminum foil and cook for 3 hours. Remove the foil, pour away all the fat (save as dripping – see page 158) and add another ¾ cup of water to the pan. Cook for 1 hour more, or until the meat falls away from the bone, adding another good splash of water if it starts to dry out.

Meanwhile, peel the potatoes, halving any larger ones, and parboil in a large saucepan of boiling salted water for 12 minutes. Drain and shake to fluff up, then tip into a roasting pan. Strip in the rest of the rosemary leaves, drizzle with oil, bash and add the remaining unpeeled garlic cloves, and toss with salt and pepper. Place in the oven under the lamb pan for the final 1 ½ hours. With 20 minutes to go, pick and very finely chop the mint leaves, scrape into a small pitcher and mix with the sugar, vinegar and 1 tablespoon of boiling water. Chop the bacon and cook in a large frying pan on a medium heat until golden. Trim, roughly slice and throw in the cabbage with a splash of water, cook for 10 to 15 minutes, or until softened, then season to perfection.

Remove the lamb from the oven, transfer to a platter and cover. Put the pan on a medium heat on the stove and stir in the flour, then pour in 2 ⅓ cups boiling water and any lamb resting juices. Stir well and simmer until you're happy with the consistency. Pour the gravy into a pitcher, or if you prefer it smooth, pour and push it through a sieve first. Quickly blanch the peas in a pan of boiling water for a couple of minutes, then drain. Serve everything in the middle of the table, with all the usual trimmings.

BAD BOY BBQ BURRITOS

LEFTOVER ...

I'm a real fan of making these burritos on the weekend because, a bit like making pizzas, everyone can add a little more or less of what they fancy, and the combination of wrap, rice, BBQ sauce, cheese and shredded meat is fantastic and always will be. Baking them in the foil is a really safe, snug way of doing it – you still achieve a little color but everything just melts inside and you get a good half an hour of hot burrito if you're on the move.

Serves 4

Total time: 40 minutes

778
calories

1 mug (10 oz) of basmati or brown rice

3 ½ oz frozen spinach

2 large red onions

2 fresh red chiles

10 oz leftover cooked lamb

1 heaping tablespoon BBQ sauce

olive oil

optional: leftover mint sauce

4 large soft flour tortillas

1 ½ oz Cheddar cheese

fat-free plain yogurt, to serve

hot chili sauce, to serve

Preheat the oven to 350°F. Cook the rice according to package instructions, then drain and return it to the saucepan. Add a pinch of salt and pepper, stir in the spinach, pop the lid on and set aside.

Meanwhile, put a grill pan on a high heat. Once hot, peel and quarter the onions, then grill and char on all sides with the chiles (prick them or they'll explode!). Remove them to a board and finely chop, removing the chile stalks and seeds. Shred over the lamb and toss together with the BBQ sauce.

Stir up the rice and spinach with a little oil and a few tablespoons of leftover mint sauce from the mothership lamb recipe, if you've got it, then season to perfection. Lay out your tortillas on four sheets of aluminum foil and divide the rice between them, covering one half of each tortilla. Line up the lamb and veg across the middle and grate over the cheese. Confidently roll up each tortilla, then wrap in the foil, twisting the ends like a Christmas cracker. Lay on a baking sheet and bake for 20 minutes, or until hot through. Cut in half and serve with yogurt and chili sauce for dipping, with a lovely fresh salad on the side.

HAPPY & HEARTY SCOTTISH BROTH

LEFTOVER...

This is the kind of meal that Scotland was founded on — it's delicious, it's nourishing, it has great depth of flavor from the lamb bones, and color and goodness from the root veg, peas and cabbage. The pearl barley and potatoes will help to fill you up, creating a hearty and homely meal that's hard to beat on the feel-good front.

Serves 6

Total time: 1 hour 30 minutes

297 calories

leftover lamb bones

7 oz leftover cooked lamb

1 chicken or beef bouillon cube

1 cup pearl barley

8 oz rutabaga

3 ½ oz turnip

2 carrots

8 oz potatoes

½ head of Savoy cabbage

¾ cup frozen peas

extra virgin olive oil

optional: leftover mint sauce

crusty bread, to serve

Put the leftover bones from the mothership lamb recipe into a large casserole pan — roughly bash them up if you can — then shred in the leftover lamb and crumble in the bouillon cube. Cover with 7 pints of water and simmer on a medium heat for 1 hour, skimming away any scum from the surface. Meanwhile, cook the pearl barley in a separate saucepan according to package instructions, then drain and put aside.

Peel the rutabaga, then chop into ½-inch dice with the turnip, carrots and potatoes (I like to leave the skin on these, as it's nutritious). Add the diced veg to the lamb pan along with the drained pearl barley and simmer for another 20 minutes. Dice the cabbage (discarding the core) and add to the broth for the last 10 minutes with the peas — the cabbage is beautiful and tasty if you keep it green and vibrant, so don't overcook it.

Scoop out the bones, then season the broth to perfection, if needed. Drizzle with a little oil and some leftover mint sauce from the mothership lamb recipe, if you have any, and serve in the middle of the table with a stack of bowls and some nice crusty bread to mop up the broth.

Like a good minestrone, this broth can take advantage of what's in season, so feel free to add a few more of your favorite veg when they're at their best and at their cheapest.

PUNCHY CRUNCHY LAMB NOODLE SALAD

LEFTOVER...

Colorful, exciting, healthy and full of big flavors and textures, this salad perfectly celebrates lovely crisp slivers of leftover roast lamb, which in turn is paired with lamb's two best mates, Mr Mint and Mr Chile. It never fails to deliver and is also happy when wodged into a little tortilla, rolled and wrapped – enjoy.

Serves 6
Total time: 25 minutes

473 calories

2 thumb-sized pieces of gingerroot

1–2 fresh red chiles

8 tablespoons olive oil

4 tablespoons red wine vinegar

4 tablespoons reduced-sodium soy sauce

10 oz medium rice noodles

2 carrots

1 English cucumber

2 heads of gem lettuce or hearts of romaine

1 head of bibb lettuce

1 bunch of fresh mint (1 oz)

8 oz leftover cooked lamb

1 tablespoon raw sesame seeds

Peel the ginger, then finely grate it with half the chile into a small bowl. Add the oil, vinegar and soy sauce to make a dressing, then put aside.

Put the noodles into a bowl, cover with boiling water and soak for around 15 minutes, or until tender, moving them about with tongs every now and then to separate them. Peel the carrots into long ribbons, erratically slice the cucumber (I'm loving my crinkle-cut knife – you should get one!), and put both into a large salad bowl. Trim the lettuces, cut into random wedges and place on top of the carrots and cucumber. Pick over the mint leaves. Drain the noodles and add to the salad bowl.

Finely slice or shred the lamb, then put into a large frying pan on a high heat with the sesame seeds. Toss together and fry for a few minutes, or until the lamb is nice and crispy and the seeds are golden.

Mix up the dressing, drizzle it over everything in the salad bowl and toss together until well coated. Finely slice the remaining chile and scatter over, then top with the crispy sesame lamb and serve right away.

If you go to your greengrocer, you can get a small handful of lots of different veg by weight – such as sugar snaps or snow peas, fresh peas and radishes – making this salad even more exciting.

LOVELY LAMB PIE

Please, please have a go at this puff pastry lamb pie – it's a real show-stopper. It goes to another level because you've got the combination of flavor from the bones and leftover meat, but it also embraces great-value kidneys, and the way they're cut and slowly stewed means they're just delightful and give the most wonderful flavor to this pie filling. The celery root is another surprising and affordable flavor revelation, so enjoy.

Serves 8

Total time: 2 hours 30 minutes
(plus cooling time)

360 calories

2 red onions

2 carrots

1 small celery root

8 oz lamb kidneys

optional: 1 tablespoon leftover lamb dripping

olive oil

1 bunch of fresh thyme (1 oz)

optional: 1 fresh bay leaf

1 heaping tablespoon all-purpose flour

2 teaspoons English mustard

2 teaspoons Worcestershire sauce

optional: leftover lamb gravy and bones

8 oz leftover cooked lamb

1 x 14-oz can of lentils

10 oz puff pastry

1 large egg

Peel the onions, carrots and celery root and trim the kidneys, then chop everything into ½-inch dice and put into a large casserole pan on a medium-low heat with the lamb dripping, if you have it, or a lug of oil, a pinch of salt and plenty of pepper. Strip in the thyme leaves and add a bay leaf, if you've got one, then cook for 30 minutes, stirring regularly. Cooking it slowly like this will create the most amazing depth of flavor for the pie filling.

Stir the flour and mustard into the pan, then add the Worcestershire sauce, 6 cups of boiling water and any leftover gravy and lamb bones from the mothership lamb recipe, if you have them. Reduce to a low heat, cover and cook gently for 1 hour, or until thickened and reduced, stirring occasionally. Remove any bones, season to perfection, then remove from the heat and leave to cool. Preheat the oven to 350°F.

Once the pie filling is cool, shred the lamb into the pan, then drain and add the lentils and mix well. Tip into a pie dish (roughly 10 x 12 inches). On a flour-dusted surface, roll out the pastry so it's slightly bigger than your dish and roughly ⅛ inch thick, then score very lightly in a criss-cross fashion. Beat the egg and brush around the rim of the dish. Roll the pastry around your rolling pin and unroll over the dish. Press to stick, then brush the pastry with more eggwash and bake for 30 to 40 minutes at the bottom of the oven, or until the filling is piping hot and the pastry is golden brown. Delicious served with seasonal greens and an extra dollop of mustard.

If you don't have leftover lamb, you can still make this pie – just use quality stewing lamb instead and pop it in with the kidneys at the start of the recipe, making sure it's tender before adding your pie lid.

CRISPY MOROCCAN LAMB PASTILLA

LEFTOVER...

Pretty much every day in the markets of Marrakesh you'll see sweet and savory pastillas being made and sold for very little money, often with pigeon, quail, goat or, as in this case, lamb, which is big over there. This is a simplified version of that dish that still delivers on flavor and, of course, uses leftovers to make it super cheap. These are to the Moroccans what Cornish pasties and pork pies are to the British – and just as tasty!

Serves 4
Total time: 1 hour 10 minutes

540 calories

½ cup couscous

2 onions

4 cloves garlic

2 oz sultanas

olive oil

1 teaspoon ground turmeric

½ teaspoon cumin seeds

8 oz leftover cooked lamb

2 ½ oz feta cheese

4 large sheets of phyllo pastry

1 tablespoon sliced almonds
  or raw sesame seeds

1 heaping teaspoon confectioner's sugar

½ teaspoon ground cinnamon

4 tablespoons fat-free plain
  yogurt, to serve

1 tablespoon harissa or chili oil, to serve

Pop the couscous into a small bowl, just cover with boiling water, then put a plate on top and leave for 10 minutes. Peel and finely chop the onions and garlic along with the sultanas and place in a large saucepan on a medium heat with a lug of oil, the turmeric and cumin seeds. Fry for around 15 minutes, or until softened, stirring occasionally. Finely shred the lamb, add to the pan and cook for a further 5 minutes, then remove the pan from the heat. Fluff up the couscous and stir it through the lamb mixture with the crumbled feta, then season to perfection, going heavy on the black pepper.

Preheat the oven to 350°F. Working fairly quickly, as phyllo dries out easily, lay out the pastry sheets on a clean work surface and brush with oil. Divide the lamb mixture between them, laying it along the shortest edge of each sheet. Roll each one up halfway, fold in the sides, then continue rolling up like big cigars. Place them on a non-stick baking sheet, brush the tops with a little oil and crumble over the almonds, or sprinkle with the sesame seeds. Sieve over the confectioner's sugar and cinnamon from a height, then bake for around 25 minutes, or until golden and crisp. Serve with yogurt, rippled with harissa or chili oil, for dipping. Delicious with a simple green salad on the side.

Feel free to mix any leftover meat with these beautiful Moroccan flavors – whatever you've got will be delicious.

INCREDIBLE LAMB BIRYANI

LEFTOVER...

Biryani is a big hitter – it's scrumptious, hearty and a bit of an Indian favorite. It has always been one of those wonderful recipes that has the capacity to use up leftovers – just like the Italians would make a lasagne, or the Brits would make a pie filling – and the flavor and moisture from the leftover shoulder of lamb is perfect for it.

Serves 6

Total time: 2 hours 30 minutes

462 calories

leftover lamb bones

2 cups basmati rice

2 thumb-sized pieces of gingerroot

6 cloves garlic

2 red onions

olive oil

optional: leftover lamb dripping

16 oz frozen spinach

1 fresh red chile

2 heaping teaspoons curry powder

2 tablespoons all-purpose flour

2 tablespoons mango chutney

red wine vinegar

8 oz leftover cooked lamb

optional: leftover lamb gravy

1 handful of sliced almonds

fat-free plain yogurt, to serve

optional: a few sprigs of fresh cilantro

Put the leftover bones from the mothership lamb recipe into a large casserole pan – roughly bash them up if you can – then cover with 6 cups of water and simmer on a medium heat for 1 hour, skimming away any scum from the surface, to make a broth. Sieve it into a large pitcher and put aside to add wicked flavor to your stew and gravy later.

Cook the rice according to package instructions, then rinse under cold water and drain. Preheat the oven to 400°F. Peel and finely chop the ginger, garlic and onions, then divide between two large saucepans, both on medium heats, with a lug of oil in each (if you've got any leftover lamb dripping from the roast, use a spoonful here instead of oil for massive flavor). Cook for 10 minutes, stirring regularly, then add the frozen spinach to one pan with a splash of water and cook down for 10 minutes, still stirring regularly, or until dark and delicious. Season to perfection and put aside. Meanwhile, finely slice the chile and stir into the second pan with the curry powder, flour, mango chutney and a splash of vinegar, then shred in the lamb. Stir well, add any leftover gravy you have from the mothership recipe, then pour in the broth and simmer for around 20 minutes, or until nice and thick. Season to perfection, then pour through a sieve into a saucepan to separate the meat stew from the gravy.

Season the rice to perfection, then layer half of it in a greased baking dish (roughly 10 x 12 inches), followed by all of the spinach and the meat stew from the sieve, finishing with a layer of rice. Sprinkle over the almonds, cover with aluminum foil and bake for around 40 minutes, or until hot through, removing the foil halfway. Serve with hot gravy and yogurt on the side, and a scattering of cilantro leaves (if using).

YOU NEED FRESH HERBS IN YOUR LIFE

GROW

It's great that we've got herbs in supermarkets, but they're expensive. If you buy from a market, they're generally half the price, and most herbs can be grown easily, for most of the year. I tend to buy soft delicate fresh herbs only if I need to, because our chilly UK weather means they don't always grow. But I have successfully grown woody herbs – rosemary, thyme, bay, oregano, sage, marjoram – and even mint, which, although a soft herb, is a loyal servant ten months of the year. Buy a container of herbs and put them in the garden, in the ground, a trough or a pot, no matter how small. All you need is a bit of soil, a bit of sun, a bit of water and a bit of love.

FOR FREE

If you're trying to save some money, look around you next time you're out. There's a massive chance you'll see rosemary, thyme, sage and bay trees that you pass every day, and honestly, a little prune, respectfully done, won't upset anyone. Just make sure you stay legal, so ask permission from the owner if the plant is on private property and don't pick anything from a nature reserve, national park or similar. And don't go crazy or uproot anything – I'm talking a few sprigs of what you need only, leaving plenty behind so the plant can recover. Also be safe! Never pick something you're unsure of – please use a field guide to be sure.

OIL

You can blend any herb with some olive oil, push it through a sieve and freeze ice-cube trays of flavored oil. Bag and label them and you can use them to start sauces, soups and stews, to make the best roast potatoes or when cooking meat or fish – the list is endless, really, and they'll be a valuable weapon in your arsenal of flavor-enhancers. You can even just pick the leaves of fresh herbs directly into the ice-cube tray, then cover them with oil and freeze.

FRESH

To keep herbs fresh for as long as possible, bunch them up, trim the stalks, then wrap them in damp paper towel and pop them into the fridge – it'll make a big difference.

BUTTER

Simply chop up fresh herbs and mash them with some peeled crushed garlic, then mix into room-temperature butter and roll it up in parchment paper like a Christmas cracker. Place in the freezer for 30 minutes to firm up, then unwrap and cut into ½-inch-thick slices. Wrap it up again and return it to the freezer until you need it – that way you'll have little discs ready for scrambled eggs, risotto, steaks, pasta, veg dishes, meat, fish, whatever you're cooking!

DRY

Drying not only preserves herbs but gives them a completely different flavor. Put them somewhere warm like an airing cupboard or next to a radiator on a rack, or simply hang them up (separate them so they dehydrate evenly). I've successfully dried basil, mint, parsley, flowering oregano and woody herbs. Dry them for at least 12 hours to maintain maximum flavor and shape. Once crisp, put them into a jar and they'll be beautiful scattered over salads, rubbed into fish or sprinkled over cheeses and antipasti platters. Not only will you waste less, they look and taste better too – triple whammy!

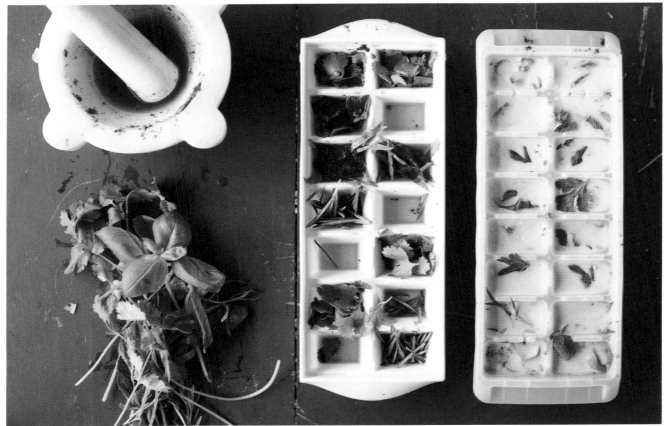

SIZZLING LAMB KOFTAS

These sizzling lamb koftas are a joy – as soon as they come off the grill they're rolled in smashed nuts and spices, before being wrapped up with pickles and crunchy veg in soft tortillas. They're super simple to make, fulfilling, and in various shapes and sizes have been the ultimate street food for hundreds of years. These are brilliant in the summer, cooked on a barbecue to really enhance that beautiful, charred smoky flavor.

Serves 4

Total time: 35 minutes

472 calories

¼ head of red cabbage

2 tablespoons white wine vinegar

1 tablespoon superfine sugar

2 oz unsalted raw pistachios

1 teaspoon fennel seeds

½ head of iceberg lettuce

2 oz stale bread

14 oz ground lamb

sweet chili sauce

4 small soft flour tortillas

8 radishes

fat-free plain yogurt, to serve

Very, very finely slice the cabbage, discarding the core, and put it into a bowl with the vinegar, sugar and a pinch of salt and pepper. Gently scrunch with your hands and put aside. Bash the pistachios and fennel seeds in a pestle and mortar or blitz in a food processor until fairly fine, then sprinkle over a board and put to one side, ready to go. Slice the lettuce.

Blitz the bread into bread crumbs in a food processor with a pinch of salt and pepper and put into a bowl with the lamb. Scrunch and mix together, then divide into 4 pieces and mold each piece around a skewer into a long sausage shape – if it's a little rustic and taking on the curves of your fingers, that's all part of it (if you're cooking on a grill pan, it's best to use wooden skewers that you've soaked in water, cut to size). Get your barbecue going or put a grill pan on a high heat to get screaming hot. Add the koftas and cook to your liking – I like them just cooked through but dark golden and really sizzling on the outside. Remove from the heat, brush with sweet chili sauce, then simply roll in the nuts and spices until well coated.

Briefly warm each tortilla on the grill pan or barbecue (give it a quick wipe or brush first), then load with a slice of iceberg, a kofta, a couple of radishes and a dollop of yogurt. Squeeze the excess salty liquid out of the pickled cabbage and add a little handful of cabbage to each tortilla, then serve.

You can use this recipe to embrace other crunchy veg like carrots and onions as well as the lettuce and radishes, and add soft fresh herbs like mint and Italian parsley, if you have them.

Using flat skewers makes this much easier, as the round ones can just spin around inside the ground meat. Otherwise, I recommend putting two skewers together and molding around those, like in the picture. You could even prune some long rosemary sprigs, strip off the leaves and use those for extra flavor – and they look great too.

KING OF ALL BURGERS

This is up there with the Formula One of burgers that you can get your naughty little hands on in restaurants, burger bars and at street food stalls all over the place. I've taken the winning combo of lamb and blue cheese and hit it up with crunchy apple, spinach, quick pickled red onion and jalapeños, and it eats like . . . a . . . dream.

Serves 4
Total time: 20 minutes

1 red onion

red wine vinegar

1 lb ground lamb

1 ½ oz Stilton cheese

4 burger buns

1 apple

tomato ketchup

optional: 1 large handful of baby spinach

optional: pickled jalapeños

These patties work well made with pork, beef, game or even a blend, instead of lamb, if you fancy. And if you don't have blue cheese, a chunk of Cheddar will be just as delicious.

Peel the onion, ideally finely slice on a mandolin (use the guard!) or by hand using good knife skills, and put into a bowl with a lug of vinegar and a good pinch of salt. Toss and scrunch together to make a quick pickle. Put aside.

Place a grill pan on a high heat to get screaming hot. Scrunch the ground lamb for 30 seconds, then divide into four. Mold into patties the same size as your burger buns (they'll shrink a bit when they cook) and season with salt and pepper. Cook on the hot grill pan for 4 minutes, then flip over, divide and immediately crumble over the Stilton, and cook for another 4 minutes, or until the burgers are charred and just cooked through, loosely covered with aluminum foil to melt the cheese.

Meanwhile, cut the burger buns in half and lightly toast them. Finely slice the apple (I'm loving my crinkle-cut knife – you should get one!), then, when you're ready to go, spread the bottoms of the buns with a little ketchup, add a couple of slices of apple, then a wodge of spinach and some pickled jalapeños, if you've got them. Top with the cheesy burgers, squeeze all the excess salty liquid out of the onions and divide between them, then pop the tops on (adding an extra blob of ketchup, if you like). Gently press down, sing two verses of your national anthem – enough to allow the delicious juices to soak into the bun – then go forward and conquer the king of all burgers. Hurrah.

CYPRIOT LAMB KEBABS

Homemade kebabs are a real treat to make, and they're just screaming out for a barbecue, although you can of course use a grill pan to great effect. Kebabs have always been brilliant for mixing the more expensive cuts of meat with cheaper ones and with things like bread to soak up all the cooking juices. Take the time to cut up anything going on the skewer to a similar size, so it all gets even contact with the heat. Beautiful.

Serves 4

Total time: 45 minutes

(plus marinating time)

478 calories

5 oz lamb livers

2 cloves garlic

1 heaping teaspoon ground coriander

1 heaping teaspoon dried oregano

1 level teaspoon sweet paprika

1 lemon

olive oil

8 oz lamb neck fillet

3 thick slices of stale bread

optional: 12–16 fresh bay leaves

2 scallions

½ English cucumber

2 ripe tomatoes

1 head of bibb lettuce

½ bunch of fresh mint (½ oz)

red wine vinegar

extra virgin olive oil

1 cup sprouted cress

4 pita breads

optional: fat-free plain yogurt, to serve

Soak the livers in a bowl of water for a few minutes. Peel the garlic and pound to a paste in a pestle and mortar. Add the ground coriander, oregano and paprika, finely grate in the lemon zest, squeeze in half the juice, then muddle in 3 tablespoons of olive oil. Chop the lamb and bread into 1-inch chunks and the drained livers into ¾-inch chunks, then toss in the marinade and leave covered for at least 1 hour, or preferably (for the best flavor) overnight in the fridge.

When you're ready to cook, get your barbecue going or put a grill pan on a high heat to get screaming hot. If using a grill pan, make sure your skewers are the right size for your pan (if wooden, soak in water to stop them burning), then, with a bit of pride, skewer up the marinated lamb, livers and bread on 4 skewers (I like to add 3 or 4 bay leaves to each skewer in between the pieces because as they burn they add great flavor). Cook the kebabs to your liking, turning until they're beautifully golden all over.

Meanwhile, trim the scallions and chop along with the rest of the salad veg and the mint leaves on a large board, mixing as you go. Add a drizzle of vinegar, twice as much extra virgin olive oil and a pinch of salt and pepper, and keep chopping and mixing until it's the consistency you like, then top with pinches of cress. Serve the kebabs and salad in a large tray with toasted pita breads and yogurt (if using), and an extra sprinkle of paprika, then let everyone build their own pita.

For sure you can get disposable wooden skewers, but I like the long rustic metal ones – invest in a decent set and you'll use them forever.

• FISH RECIPES •

Reconnecting with your fishmonger, understanding how to make the most of cooking with fresh fish, knowing what your supermarket is good for and finding that balance of using good frozen and farmed fish where appropriate is what I've tried to demonstrate throughout this chapter. The recipes are varied, exciting and delicious, and illustrate how to embrace each of these options. Sustainability is a big issue, and we humans have done a great job of overfishing certain areas, so it's always good to be aware of this when you're shopping. Hugh Fearnley-Whittingstall is doing a great job raising awareness about it, so it's worth visiting his website, fishfight.net, for really up-to-date info. To do your bit, look out for MSC-approved fish, or speak to your fishmonger about what's responsibly sourced.

Mothership roast salmon

Salmon is regularly on sale at the market or supermarket, so you can often get a great deal on a whole side – this is simply one of the realities of supply and demand with fish, where there are sometimes surpluses. Anyway, use this as an opportunity to cook a whole side, which is epic, exciting and will give you amazing leftovers that I'll show you how to use up in other delicious meals in the days that follow.

Serves 6 plus leftovers

Total time: 45 minutes

 495 calories

1 x 3 ½-lb side of salmon, skin on, scaled and pin-boned

olive oil

6 sprigs of fresh rosemary

2 ½ lbs baby white potatoes

1 heaping teaspoon Dijon mustard

extra virgin olive oil

red or white wine vinegar

2 heads of bibb lettuce

6 heaping tablespoons fat-free plain yogurt

½ bunch of fresh dill (½ oz) or 1 heaping teaspoon dried dill

1 ½ oz feta cheese

1 lemon

Check that the salmon is scaled before you start cooking, so you can make use of the delicious skin.

Preheat the oven to 400°F. Put the salmon into a large roasting pan, skin-side up, and drizzle with olive oil (if I've got a jar of sun-dried tomatoes open, I like to use a bit of tasty oil from there instead, for free added flavor). Add a pinch of salt and pepper and rub all over the salmon, then strip over the rosemary leaves. Roast at the top of the oven for around 25 minutes, or until cooked through.

Meanwhile, scrub the potatoes and cook in a large saucepan of boiling salted water for 20 to 25 minutes, or until cooked through (timings will depend on the size and how fresh the potatoes are). Put the mustard and 2 tablespoons each of extra virgin olive oil and vinegar into a bowl with a pinch of salt and pepper and mix. Wash the lettuce leaves whole (trimming the base), shake dry and scatter over a platter. Drizzle over the dressing.

Drain the potatoes and leave to steam dry while you mix the yogurt with a drizzle of extra virgin olive oil and a splash of vinegar. Chop and add the dill, then toss with the potatoes, season to perfection and tip onto a second platter. Crumble the feta over the potatoes and lettuce.

Remove the salmon to another nice platter (you can serve it hot or at room temperature). Carefully peel off the salmon skin in one piece and put it back into the pan upside down, return it to the oven for a few minutes until golden and crispy, then lay it back on the salmon – when it cools, it'll be crisp and delicious. Serve with the dressed baby potatoes and lettuce, with lemon wedges on the side for squeezing over.

LEFTOVER...

Tasty salmon tacos

I love soft warm tacos that wrap up exciting things and have hidden pops of flavor. Playing with texture and temperature – soft and crunchy, hot and cold – will ensure they're a complete pleasure to eat. I've given you the recipe for making your own tacos here, which is a really lovely thing to do, rather than always using storebought ones.

Serves 6

Total time: 45 minutes

393 calories

1 ⅔ cups all-purpose flour, plus extra

    for dusting

olive oil

½ red onion

¼ English cucumber

2 tablespoons white wine vinegar

2 ripe avocados

6 tablespoons fat-free plain yogurt

2 limes

1 bunch of fresh mint (1 oz)

optional: leftover salmon skin

13 oz leftover cooked salmon

optional: hot chili sauce

Place the flour in a large bowl with a pinch of salt and make a well in the middle. Add 2 tablespoons of oil and ⅔ cup of water to the well and use a fork to bring in the flour and mix together. When it comes together into a dough, tip it onto a flour-dusted surface, knead until smooth, then divide into 12 balls and cover with a clean damp kitchen towel.

Peel and very finely slice the red onion, cut the cucumber into chunky matchsticks, put them into a bowl with the vinegar and a good pinch of salt, then scrunch together and put aside. Squidge the avocado flesh into a bowl, discarding the pit and skin, then add the yogurt and the juice from 1 lime. Pick and finely chop half the mint leaves (save the rest for garnish), then mash it all together with a fork or blender, and put to one side.

Roll one of the dough balls out nice and thin, turning as you go and dusting with a little extra flour if needed, until you have a perfect circle (roughly 6 inches in diameter). Put a frying pan on a medium heat and cook the taco for 1 minute on each side (with very little color, so it's soft and flexible). Roll the next one out while the previous one is cooking, stacking them in foil as you go so they stay warm. If you have any leftover salmon skin, crisp it up in the pan for a couple of minutes at the end.

Squeeze the excess salty liquid out of the quick pickle, then take everything to the table. Let everyone load up their own tacos with smashed avocado, a little handful of the pickle, a few flakes of leftover salmon, some bits of crispy skin (if you have them), chili sauce (if you like), a few extra mint leaves and a squeeze of lime juice. Heaven in a mouthful.

Salmon – 4 beautiful ways

LEFTOVER...

Here are my four favorite simple ways to create wonderfully quick salmon brunches, lunches or suppers.

Salmon & scrambled eggs

393 calories

Serves 2

Total time: 5 to 10 minutes

Crack 4 large eggs into a bowl and beat them with a pinch of salt and pepper. Heat a frying pan on a medium heat, add a splash of olive oil and 1 small knob of unsalted butter, then pour in the eggs and stir with a spatula around every 15 seconds until you have sheets of silky soft scrambled egg. Meanwhile, toast 2 nice slices of bread, then drizzle with extra virgin olive oil. Spoon the scrambled eggs on top, divide and flake over 3 ½ oz of leftover cooked salmon, sprinkle with black pepper, add a good squeeze of lemon juice and serve. Nice with a few drips of Tabasco sauce.

Simple salmon sarnie

358 calories

Serves 1

Total time: 5 minutes

Put 1 tablespoon of quality mayonnaise or fat-free plain yogurt into a bowl with 1 level teaspoon of English mustard or jarred grated horseradish (whichever you prefer), a pinch of salt and pepper, and a good squeeze of lemon juice. Finely chop and add 2 sprigs of fresh dill or a good pinch of dried dill (if you have it), then mix together. Lightly butter 2 slices of nice fresh or toasted bread, flake over 2 oz of leftover cooked salmon, dot with the spiked mayonnaise or yogurt, add a wedge of watercress, then squeeze the sandwich together and attack it at will.

Salmon-topped jacket spuds

334 calories

Serves 4

Total time: 1 hour 5 minutes

Preheat the oven to 375°F. Wash 4 baking potatoes and stab all over with a fork. Lightly season with salt and pepper and bake for around 1 hour, or until crisp on the outside and fluffy in the middle. Finely chop ½ a bunch of fresh chives (leaving some of the long tops of the chives to garnish) and put them into a bowl along with an 8-oz container of cottage cheese, 10 oz of leftover cooked salmon and a good squeeze of lemon juice (adding a dash of Tabasco sauce, if you like), then mix together and season to perfection. Score a criss-cross in the top of the potatoes, squeeze them at the base to bust them open, then pile in the salmon topping, scatter with your reserved chives and tuck in.

Silky salmon tagliatelle

537 calories

Serves 4

Total time: 15 to 20 minutes

Cook 11 oz of dried tagliatelle in a large saucepan of boiling salted water according to package instructions. Meanwhile, pour ⅓ cup of heavy cream into a small pan, bring to a boil, then finely grate in the zest of 1 lemon and add a pinch of salt and pepper. Beat 1 large egg with 1 ½ oz of finely grated Parmesan cheese and a good squeeze of lemon juice. Reserving a cupful of cooking water, drain the pasta, then tip it back into the large saucepan and pour over the cream. Stir really well, then roughly flake in 10 oz of leftover cooked salmon and slowly add the egg mixture, constantly moving the pasta. Loosen with a splash of cooking water, if needed, and finish with an extra grating of Parmesan. Delicious with a fresh green salad.

Salmon phyllo pie

Brilliant as a lunch or light dinner, this phyllo pie looks and tastes fantastic – crisp on the outside, flaky and soft in the middle. As well as salmon, we're also celebrating slow-cooked leeks and zucchini, which do amazing things when given time to get soft and sweet. They help stretch the salmon further and complement it perfectly.

Serves 6

Total time: 1 hour 50 minutes

449 calories

3 leeks

2 large zucchini

olive oil

2 sprigs of fresh thyme

7 oz leftover cooked salmon

3 ½ oz feta cheese

1 lemon

3 large eggs

½ x 16-oz package of phyllo pastry

½ oz Parmesan cheese

1 head of romaine lettuce

1 English cucumber

3 tablespoons extra virgin olive oil

Trim and roughly chop the leeks and zucchini and place in a large saucepan on a low heat with a lug of olive oil and the thyme leaves. Cook gently for 30 minutes, or until soft and lightly golden, with the lid on for the first 15 minutes, stirring regularly. Once soft and sweet, season to perfection and leave aside to cool for 5 to 10 minutes.

Preheat the oven to 350°F. Flake the salmon into the cooled mixture, crumble in the feta, grate over the zest from the lemon, crack in the eggs and stir well to combine. Layer the phyllo over the base of a lightly oiled ovenproof frying pan or dish (roughly 12 inches in diameter), overlapping the sheets and letting them hang over the edge of the pan as you layer – make sure you fully cover the base and allow enough overhang to fully cover the filling once folded in – brushing with olive oil as you go. Spoon in the salmon filling, then fold in the overhanging phyllo to form a lid. Brush the top with olive oil and finely grate over the Parmesan. Bake on the bottom shelf of the oven for 45 to 50 minutes, or until cooked through, golden and crisp.

Meanwhile, slice the lettuce and cucumber (I'm loving my crinkle-cut knife – you should get one!). Mix the juice from the lemon, the extra virgin olive oil and a pinch of salt and pepper together, then drizzle over the salad veg. Transfer the phyllo pie to a board, cut into wedges and serve.

To make this pie extra cute, try tossing a few thyme sprigs in oil and scattering them over the phyllo before you bake it.

Kinda Vietnamese salmon salad

LEFTOVER...

Back in the day, the French colonizers had a big influence on Vietnamese cuisine, so I've brought those two styles together to make brilliant use of leftover salmon in this delicious salad. With lots of crunchy veg, flaky salmon and a gorgeous dressing, it's super simple, and the little slivers of apple add something magical.

Serves 4

Total time: 30 minutes

458 calories

7 oz ciabatta or stale bread

olive oil

optional: leftover salmon skin

7 oz fresh or frozen green beans

1 thumb-sized piece of gingerroot

½–1 fresh red chile

4 tablespoons extra virgin olive oil

3 tablespoons white wine vinegar

1 tablespoon reduced-sodium soy sauce

1 English cucumber

1 bunch of radishes

2 heads of gem lettuce or hearts of romaine

2 apples

10 oz leftover cooked salmon

Preheat the oven to 350°F. Rip the bread into large rustic croutons or chop into ¾-inch chunks, drizzle with olive oil and place on a pan in the oven for around 20 minutes, or until golden and crispy (if you've got any salmon skin left over from the mothership recipe, pop it in the oven with the croutons to crisp up). Meanwhile, if using fresh beans, trim and halve. Blanch the beans in a large pan of boiling salted water for around 6 minutes if using fresh, or just a couple of minutes if using frozen, until tender. Drain and allow to cool for a minute.

Peel the ginger and finely grate into a bowl with the chile. Add the extra virgin olive oil, vinegar and soy sauce, mix together and put to one side. Halve the cucumber lengthways, scrape out the watery core, then dice, halve the radishes, cut the lettuces into erratic chunks, finely slice the apples on a mandolin (use the guard!), or by hand using really good knife skills, and put it all into a nice serving bowl with the crispy croutons and salmon skin (if using). Add the beans to the salad and flake in the salmon. Drizzle the dressing over everything, toss together really well and serve straight away.

Sweet pea fish pie

Fish pie is one of my favorites and seems to be one of yours too, so I've written this new recipe to be super thrifty and make use of your freezer staples – and I have to say, it's one of my best (using smashed sweet peas in the mash is a revelation). In theory, fish pies have always been about stretching fish a long way, and by using quality frozen fish fillets you can get in any supermarket, it's unbelievable how cheaply you can make it.

Serves 8

Total time: 1 hour 30 minutes

2 lbs potatoes

1 lemon

3 tablespoons unsalted butter

2 ¾ cups frozen peas

2 carrots

2 onions

olive oil

2 cups reduced-fat (2%) milk

2 x 5-oz frozen salmon fillets

2 x 3 ½-oz frozen white fish fillets

6 tablespoons all-purpose flour

3 ½ oz frozen spinach

4 oz frozen cooked peeled shrimp

1 heaping teaspoon English mustard

1 ½ oz Cheddar cheese

Preheat the oven to 350°F. Peel the potatoes and cut into large even-sized chunks, then put them into a large saucepan of boiling salted water for 15 minutes, or until cooked through. Drain and mash with a pinch of salt and pepper, the zest from the lemon and the butter. Place the frozen peas in a colander, pour over some boiling water to defrost them, then drain well and pulse a few times in a food processor. Fold them through the mashed potato to create a rippled effect, then leave to one side.

Peel and chop the carrots and onions and cook them in a large ovenproof pan (roughly 12 inches in diameter) with a lug of oil for 15 minutes, or until softened but not colored, stirring occasionally. Meanwhile, heat the milk in a saucepan on a medium heat. Once simmering, add all the frozen fish fillets for around 10 minutes, or until cooked through, then use a slotted spoon to remove them to a plate, taking the pan off the heat.

Stir the flour into the carrots and onions, then gradually add the milk, a ladleful at a time, stirring continuously. Stir in the spinach until broken down, then season to perfection. Flake in the fish fillets (carefully remove and discard the skin if the fillets have it), add the shrimp, mustard and the juice from half the lemon, grate in the Cheddar and stir gently to combine. Top with the pea-spiked mash and smooth out, scuffing it up slightly with a fork to give it great texture. Bake for 30 to 40 minutes, or until beautifully golden. Serve with a good old helping of baked beans (if you like) – delicious!

Fantastic fish tikka curry

Knocking out a perfumed, delicious fish curry with fluffy rice, loads of veggies and explosions of flavor is a fairly regular thing in the Oliver household – we all love it (apart from Buddy, he's still in training). This is a cracking version, and in the spirit of keeping costs down, a wonderful opportunity to embrace quality frozen fish, which is perfect here, as well as frozen cauliflower – both great-value products.

Serves 4

Total time: 1 hour 10 minutes

 523 calories

1 lemon

3 tablespoons tikka curry paste

14 oz frozen white fish fillets

1 onion

2 cloves garlic

1 thumb-sized piece of gingerroot

1 fresh red chile

½ bunch of fresh cilantro (½ oz)

olive oil

10 oz potatoes

2 ripe tomatoes

10 oz frozen cauliflower florets

2 oz dried split red lentils

1 mug (10 oz) of basmati rice

10 whole cloves

4 tablespoons fat-free plain yogurt

Cut the lemon in half, cut one half into wedges for serving later, then squeeze the juice of the other half onto a large plate and add 1 tablespoon of tikka paste. Mix together, then massage all over the frozen fish and leave aside in a single layer to marinate and defrost.

Peel and slice the onion, garlic and ginger with the chile and cilantro stalks, then place it all in a large casserole pan on a medium heat with a lug of oil and the remaining tikka paste. Peel the potatoes, cut them into ¾-inch chunks, then stir them into the pan and cook everything for 15 minutes, or until softened, stirring occasionally. This will build up great flavor.

Quarter the tomatoes, add to the pan with the cauliflower, lentils and 2 ⅓ cups of boiling water, and bring back to a boil. Simmer for 45 minutes, or until the lentils are cooked through and the sauce is lovely and thick, adding splashes of water, if needed, then season to perfection.

Around 15 minutes before the curry is ready, put 1 mug of rice and 2 mugs of boiling water into a pan with a pinch of salt and the cloves. Cook on a medium heat, with the lid on, for 12 minutes, or until all the liquid has been absorbed. Dry-fry the fish in a large non-stick frying pan for 3 to 5 minutes per side (depending on the thickness), or until charred, gnarly and cooked through – don't be tempted to move it around, just let it color and crisp up nicely. Stir half the yogurt through the curry and dollop the remaining yogurt on top. Fluff up the rice, flake the fish on top, then sprinkle with cilantro leaves and serve alongside the curry, with lemon wedges for squeezing over.

Sweet & sour fish balls

This is an old Anglo-Chinese classic – it's got beautiful textures, the balls are awesome, and the sweet and sour flavors explode in your mouth. As is quite common with Chinese cooking, the ingredients list is fairly long, but don't let that put you off – this is great-value comfort food that you're guaranteed to enjoy.

Serves 6

Total time: 50 minutes

457 calories

4 oz stale bread

1 heaping tablespoon Chinese five-spice
  powder

14 oz fresh or frozen raw squid rings
  or tubes

8 oz fresh or frozen peeled raw shrimp

1 thumb-sized piece of gingerroot

1 bunch of fresh cilantro (1 oz)

1 large egg

5 tablespoons cornstarch

1 red bell pepper

1 yellow bell pepper

2 carrots

4 scallions

olive oil

1 tablespoon tomato paste

2 tablespoons reduced-sodium soy sauce

1 tablespoon hot chili sauce

2 tablespoons white wine vinegar

1 x 8-oz can of pineapple chunks in juice

½ cup frozen peas

1 mug (10 oz) basmati rice

Whiz the bread and five-spice into bread crumbs in a food processor, then tip onto a tray and put aside. Put the squid and shrimp into the processor (hold the machine steady if using frozen). Peel and add the ginger, rip in the cilantro stalks, add the egg, 3 tablespoons of cornstarch and a small pinch of salt and pepper, then blitz until smooth and place in the fridge.

Meanwhile, seed and roughly chop the peppers, peel and finely slice the carrots, and trim and slice the white part of the scallions (finely slice the green part for later). Put the veg into a large pan on a medium-low heat with a lug of oil. Cook for 10 minutes, stirring regularly, then stir in the remaining cornstarch, the tomato paste, soy and chili sauces, vinegar, pineapple (with juice) and 1 ⅔ cups of cold water. Simmer for 15 minutes, or until thickened, adding the peas for the last few minutes. Meanwhile, put 1 mug of rice and 2 mugs of boiling water into a saucepan on a medium heat and cook for 12 minutes with the lid on, or until all the liquid has been absorbed.

Spoon out heaping teaspoons of the chilled fish mixture and roll in the bread crumbs until well coated, then roll into perfect little balls. Place a large non-stick frying pan on a medium heat, add a lug of oil and fry the fish balls for around 5 minutes, or until golden all over and cooked through (you may need to do this in batches). Pour the sweet and sour veg sauce onto a nice platter, place the fish balls on top and serve with the fluffy rice. Scatter everything with the cilantro leaves and reserved scallions, then dig in.

STALE BREAD IS A BEAUTIFUL THING

There's nothing particularly sexy about a leftover bit of stale bread, but if you think about it, some of the very best recipes in the world have been based on using it up. It can be sliced, diced, whizzed, dried, baked or flavored, to give you beautiful rustic croutons or sprinkles to use on salads, pastas, soups, risottos and stews, or it can be used inside puddings, meatloaves and burgers to make them light and stretch the expensive ingredients further.

TASTE

Unimportant as that leftover bit of stale bread might seem, I often find that customers comment on the things I make out of it, such as delicious croutons or sprinkles, because they give amazing texture and contrast to whatever they're added to, which surprises your mouth and your brain, and therefore makes you taste things even more. I like to have a mixture of my own dried bread in various forms in my kitchen arsenal.

BREAD CRUMBS

I like to food-process some really finely and some coarsely. If the bread's fresh, put the crumbs into a bag and freeze them, and if the bread's stale, simply lay them out on a tray and let them fully dry, then pack them in an airtight jar.

SUPER CRUSTY

If you've ever wondered how some Italian bread has such a beautiful crunchy base, this could be one of the oldest secrets in the bread-baking book. Instead of using flour, use fine stale bread crumbs to dust the bottom of the pan before adding your dough. It stops it sticking and gives you double the crunch.

CROUTONS

I like to make croutons three different ways. Dice bread into two sizes – ½ inch for small and 1 ¼ inches for large – or make rustic croutons by simply tearing it into thumb-sized pieces. These are all great for sprinkling over delicious salads and soups. If you've got an oven that's finished being used but is still cooling down, just whack a tray of bread in there to dry out overnight – croutons, bread crumbs, toast, whatever you fancy. It's a great way to take advantage of that free heat, as you've already paid for it! If you want to infiltrate those croutons with some serious flavor, simply toss them with some smashed-up woody herbs, garlic, spice or chile before you toast them.

TOASTS

Finely slice some bread, lay it out on a pan and either leave it to go completely stale, or, if you want to develop a little bit more flavor, pop it into the oven to achieve a little color and let it dry out. Either way, store your toasts in an airtight jar or container until you need them. They'll be really nice with cheese, pâté, pickles, hummus or guacamole, or even reheated and snapped into salads to act like croutons.

Cajun salmon & shrimp fishcakes

These Cajun fishcakes are super cute, crispy on the outside, soft in the middle and have just enough spice to get your tastebuds going. To complement them perfectly I've given you a zingy chopped salad, and the condiment of choice, strangely for me (Mr Rustic), is a quenelled teaspoon of horseradish, which works really, really well.

Serves 6

Total time: 1 hour 40 minutes

(plus defrosting time)

 321 calories

7 oz frozen salmon fillets

7 oz frozen peeled cooked shrimp

1 lb potatoes

1 fresh red chile

2 lemons

2 ½ oz ciabatta or stale bread

1 heaping tablespoon Cajun seasoning

olive oil

2 tablespoons all-purpose flour

1 head of iceberg lettuce

1 English cucumber

4 medium-sized ripe tomatoes

optional: ½ bunch of fresh dill (½ oz)
    or 1 heaping teaspoon dried dill

2 tablespoons red wine vinegar

4 tablespoons extra virgin olive oil

6 teaspoons grated horseradish (from a jar)

Start by defrosting the salmon and shrimp, preferably overnight in the fridge, covered on the bottom shelf.

Peel the potatoes and cut into large even-sized chunks, then put them into a saucepan of boiling salted water for 15 minutes, or until cooked through. Drain and leave to steam dry, then mash well in a bowl and leave to cool. Carefully remove and discard the salmon skin, if the fillets have it, then roughly chop with the shrimp. Seed and finely chop the chile and add it to the mash with the fish, shrimp, a pinch of salt and pepper and the finely grated zest from half a lemon. Mix well, divide into 6 pieces, and shape each one into a patty about ¾ inch thick.

Whiz the bread, Cajun seasoning and a lug of olive oil in a food processor to make fine bread crumbs, then tip onto a plate. Mix the flour with 2 tablespoons of water to form a loose paste, then brush over one side of the fishcakes. Gently press into the bread crumbs until well coated, then brush the other side and do the same, transferring them to an oiled pan as you go. Cover with plastic wrap and pop into the fridge for 30 minutes to firm up. Meanwhile, preheat the oven to 400°F.

Bake the fishcakes for 20 to 30 minutes, or until crisp, golden and cooked through. Meanwhile, chop the lettuce, cucumber, tomatoes and dill (if using) together on a board, then dress with the vinegar, extra virgin olive oil and a pinch of salt and pepper. Divide between your plates, pop a fishcake on each portion, top with fiery horseradish (feel free to go for as much or as little as you like), and serve with the remaining lemon, cut into wedges.

Jools' sweet pea & shrimp pasta shells

This is a great, quick, last-minute lunch or dinner. All the ingredients live happily in the pantry or freezer waiting to be put together, and the combination of sweet peas, shrimp and tomato sauce is undeniably delicious. You'll notice I'm using a little Parmesan here. I know Italians often say to never use cheese with seafood, but that's not always true – I've seen it used subtly like this as a sort of seasoning and it serves a very useful purpose.

Serves 4

Total time: 15 minutes

418 calories

11 oz dried pasta shells

4 cloves garlic

1 fresh red chile

olive oil

7 oz frozen peeled cooked shrimp

1 ½ cups frozen peas

1 heaping tablespoon tomato paste

1 oz Parmesan cheese

Cook the pasta in a large saucepan of boiling salted water according to package instructions. Meanwhile, peel and finely slice the garlic, seed and finely slice the chile, then put both into a large frying pan on a medium heat with a lug of oil. Fry until lightly golden, then stir in the shrimp, peas and tomato paste, add a few swigs of boiling cooking water from the pasta pan, and simmer slowly on a low heat until the pasta is ready.

Once cooked, drain the pasta, reserving a cupful of cooking water. Season the sauce to perfection, then toss with the pasta. Finely grate over the Parmesan and mix together, loosening with a little cooking water, if needed. Divide between your bowls and serve right away.

This simple recipe is super versatile and is also delicious made with gently simmered squid, baby shrimp, or, if you can find it on a good deal, fresh cooked crab meat in place of the shrimp.

Grilled garlic mussels
Sweet tomato soup

This is an unusual but absolutely brilliant dish. You've got a really homely and delicious, simple tomato soup, and to go alongside it, garlicky meaty mussels topped with crispy bread crumbs. It's a great combination, really fun to do, totally affordable, and people just love bouncing from one to the other when you serve it up.

Serves 4

Total time: 45 minutes

1 small red onion

4 cloves garlic

olive oil

½ teaspoon fennel seeds

½ teaspoon dried chili flakes

2 x 14-oz cans of diced tomatoes

2 lbs mussels, washed and debearded

3 ½ oz stale bread

1 ½ oz Cheddar cheese

½ bunch of fresh Italian parsley (½ oz)

Preheat the broiler to high. Peel and finely chop the onion and 2 cloves of garlic, then put them into a large saucepan on a medium heat with a lug of oil. Add the fennel seeds and chili flakes and cook for 5 minutes, or until softened. Tip in the tomatoes and add 2 cans' worth of water, season with black pepper, bring to a boil, then simmer for 20 minutes.

Meanwhile, put the mussels and a splash of water into another large saucepan on a high heat (tap any mussels that are open and if they don't close, throw those ones away). Pop the lid on and cook, shaking after a couple of minutes, until all the mussels have opened (throw away any that remain closed) – don't be tempted to overcook them, they should be plump and juicy. Hold a sieve over the soup and drain the mussels – in batches, if necessary – so all the liquid goes into the soup to add extra flavor.

Tip the mussels into a large roasting pan, then snap the top shells off, leaving the bottom shells and meaty mussels behind. Spread them out in one layer. Tear the bread into a food processor, add the Cheddar, the remaining garlic (peeled), the parsley (stalks and all) and a lug of oil, then blitz into rough bread crumbs. Evenly scatter them over the mussels and pop under the broiler for 5 to 8 minutes, or until crisp and golden. Blitz the soup with an immersion blender, season to perfection and serve on the side.

Carbonara of smoked mackerel

This is a lovely twist in the tale of a traditional carbonara that uses smoked fish instead of bacon. For me, it's the subtle emulsion of cooking water, eggs and Parmesan that gives that really comforting carbonara experience, along with something smoky – in this case the lovely mackerel – and lots of black pepper.

Serves 4
Total time: 25 minutes

543 calories

11 oz dried penne

1 onion

1 large zucchini

2 sprigs of fresh rosemary

4 ½ oz smoked boneless mackerel fillets

olive oil

2 large eggs

⅓ cup reduced-fat (2%) milk

1 ½ oz Parmesan cheese

optional: 1 lemon

Cook the penne in a saucepan of boiling salted water according to package instructions. Meanwhile, peel and finely slice the onion, then cut the zucchini into quarters lengthways and cut out the fluffy core. Slice the zucchini at an angle, roughly ½ inch thick – you want the pieces to be about the same size and shape as the penne. Pick and chop the rosemary leaves, then slice the mackerel ½ inch thick (removing the skin, if you like). Put the onions and zucchini into a large frying pan on a medium heat with a lug of oil and a pinch of salt and pepper, stirring occasionally. After 5 minutes, add the rosemary and mackerel and cook for a further 5 minutes, or until nice and golden, tossing occasionally.

Meanwhile, whisk the eggs and milk together, then finely grate in the Parmesan. Reserving a cupful of cooking water, drain the pasta and toss it into the mackerel pan. Take the pan off the heat for a few seconds and stir in a good splash of the reserved water to cool it down (this is really important, because if you add your eggs when the pan's still screaming hot, the heat will simply scramble them – you want the sauce to be silky smooth). Quickly pour in the egg mixture and shake and stir together until thickened, silky and evenly coated, then plate up and serve with an extra grating of Parmesan, a good pinch of pepper and a squeeze of lemon juice, if you like.

KNOW YOUR ...
FISHMONGER

This lovely fella, Dan Eastwood, is my local mobile fishmonger in Essex. I know I can call on him any day and he'll advise me on what's in season, what's been caught, what's local, what's farmed and, very importantly these days, what's sustainable, as fish is quite literally a moving target and the politics change regularly. Here are our top tips about buying fish:

1 Get to know your fishmonger on first-name terms — they're your ally and want to keep your custom.

2 Tell your fishmonger what your budget is and how much you've got to spend per person, and they'll work to it.

3 Really fresh fish always has shiny skin, bright eyes, firm, flashy red gills and smells of the sea — it shouldn't smell fishy.

4 Fresh fish is best eaten on the day you buy it. Shop when you need it and you'll never hear the word "fishy" again.

5 Be more open-minded about the fish you eat — don't always go for cod or haddock. Your fishmonger can advise you, and it'll normally be cheaper too!

6 Tuesday to Saturday are the best fish days, as fishermen have the weekends off, but of course, that doesn't mean you can't get fresh farmed fish every day of the week.

7 Most modern fishmongers will tweet or Facebook about what's fresh and available, and from that, plan your recipes, not the other way around. Or, keep it old-school and simply give them a call to find out what they've got in.

SHOP
SMART

My favorite Sicilian sardine spaghetti

I'm fully aware that this isn't your everyday pasta, but it's sumptuously gorgeous and will put big smiles on people's faces. Sardines are super cheap and something we should all embrace and eat more of – simply get your fishmonger to remove the scales, fillet them and remove the main bones, and you're going to cook up a storm.

Serves 4
Total time: 50 minutes

2 onions

½ bunch of fresh Italian parsley (½ oz)

olive oil

1 teaspoon fennel seeds

½–1 teaspoon dried chili flakes

1 x 14-oz can of diced tomatoes

1 lemon

4 fresh sardines, scaled, filleted and pin-boned

extra virgin olive oil

11 oz dried spaghetti

Peel the onions, finely chop with the parsley stalks and put into a large frying pan on a low heat with a lug of olive oil, the fennel seeds and chili flakes. Cook gently for around 20 minutes, or until really soft and sticky, stirring occasionally, to create a great base for the sauce.

Tip in the tomatoes (I quite like the tomato element to be silky smooth, so I blend the tomatoes or push them through a sieve before adding them) and half a can's worth of water, then bring to a boil. Grate in the lemon zest, then simmer gently for another 20 minutes, stirring occasionally. Season the sauce to perfection, then lay the sardines skin-side up on top and drizzle with a little extra virgin olive oil. Pop the lid on and simmer for just 5 minutes – that's enough to cook them through.

Meanwhile, cook the spaghetti in a large saucepan of boiling salted water according to package instructions. Finely chop the parsley leaves. Reserving a cupful of cooking water, drain the spaghetti and add it to the sardine sauce with the parsley leaves and a squeeze of lemon juice. Toss together, loosening with cooking water, if needed, then divide between your plates and serve right away, with a crisp green salad on the side.

To take this dish even further (like in the picture), because it's a Sicilian recipe it's particularly good if you sprinkle pine nuts and bread crumbs over the top of the raw sardines, then place under the broiler for 3 to 5 minutes (depending on their size), until lovely and crispy. This adds terrific texture when you toss it all together.

Trout al forno

I love a bit of trout al forno. It's one of those dinners that's really straightforward to put together but makes it look like you've put in a lot of effort. Crispy potatoes and squash, sweet onion, flaky trout with mustard and oats on the skin, whack that in the middle of the table, let everyone help themselves and it's happy days.

Serves 4

Total time: 1 hour 20 minutes

502 calories

1 butternut squash

1 ¾ lbs potatoes

1 large onion

olive oil

½ bunch of fresh thyme (½ oz)

1 slice of stale bread (2 oz)

1 clove garlic

1 heaping tablespoon oats

3 ½ oz rainbow trout fillets,
    skin on, scaled and pin-boned

1 teaspoon English mustard

a few sprigs of fresh rosemary

Preheat the oven to 400°F. Seed the squash, then peel and carefully slice it ¼ inch thick, along with the potatoes and onion (if you want to save time and make it a bit healthier, leave the skins on the squash and potato). Put it all into the largest pan that will fit inside your oven, toss in a little oil, salt and pepper and strip over the thyme leaves, then spread out evenly. Roast on the bottom shelf of the oven for 50 to 60 minutes, or until lightly golden and a little crispy.

Whiz the bread, peeled garlic and a lug of oil in a food processor to make bread crumbs, then pulse in the oats, simply to mix them through, and put aside. When the time's up, remove the pan from the oven and lay the trout fillets on top, skin-side up. Brush a stripe of mustard across the center of the trout fillets, then lightly scatter over the oaty crumbs. Drizzle any exposed fish with a little oil, then strip the rosemary leaves, toss in oil and scatter over the veg. Roast for 12 to 14 minutes, or until golden. Delicious served with a simple lemony-dressed green salad or spring greens.

This recipe also works really well with sardines or striped bass fillets. Ask your fishmonger to advise you on what's in season and the best value.

Mussel pasta e fagioli

Pasta e fagioli is classic Italian peasant food. It varies in consistency around the country, a little soupier in central Italy, getting thicker in the south. Various pasta shapes can be used, so it's a great way to use up any odds and ends. In this expression, mussels, which are incredible value, a great source of protein and definitely something we should be eating more of, give incredible depth of flavor and make it taste and look exciting.

Serves 6

Total time: 1 hour

385 calories

6 rashers of smoked bacon

olive oil

1 large onion

3 cloves garlic

½ bunch of fresh Italian parsley (½ oz)

3 carrots

1 good pinch of dried chili flakes

1 x 14-oz can of diced tomatoes

1 x 14-oz can of cannellini beans

1 lemon

10 oz mixed dried pasta shapes

2 lbs mussels, washed and debearded

extra virgin olive oil

Chop the bacon and place in a large saucepan on a medium heat with a drizzle of olive oil to get golden, stirring occasionally, while you peel and finely chop the onion and garlic with the parsley stalks, and peel and slice the carrots. Add these to the pan with the chili flakes and cook for 15 minutes, or until softened, still stirring occasionally.

Add the tomatoes and beans (juice and all) to the pan, then pour in 5 cups of boiling water. Bring to a boil, then reduce to a simmer for 20 minutes, or until fairly thick, stirring occasionally.

Taste the sauce, add a squeeze of lemon juice, then season to perfection. Add the pasta and cook for 7 minutes, then pile the mussels on top of the sauce (tap any that are open and if they don't close, throw those ones away). Pop the lid on and cook for 5 more minutes, or until all the mussels have just opened (throw away any that remain closed) and the pasta is cooked through. Toss the mussels through the sauce, then chop the parsley leaves and scatter over. Finish with a little drizzle of extra virgin olive oil and serve right away. Nice with a crisp green salad.

Tuna melt piadina

People love a piadina, especially in northern Italy – it's basically a toasted flatbread filled with something delicious. In this recipe, Italy meets classic college fodder, and honestly, in its own cute way, it's artisanal and will get your tastebuds going. If you want to round it off nicely, a simple salad on the side is perfect.

Serves 2 to 4

Total time: 40 minutes

711 calories

2 cups self-rising flour, plus extra for dusting

olive oil

1 small red onion

1 apple

white wine vinegar

1 x 6-oz can of tuna in spring water

1 oz Cheddar cheese

2 tablespoons reduced-fat cream cheese

English mustard

optional: Tabasco sauce

Place the flour in a bowl with ½ cup of water, mix together with a fork until it starts to come together, then go in with your hands and pat and bring it all into a dough. Knead for a few minutes, adding a little more flour if too wet or a splash more water if too dry. Divide into 2 balls and flatten each piece to roughly 7 inches wide. Put a splash of oil into a medium non-stick frying pan on a medium heat and add one piece of the flattened dough, rubbing a little oil on the top. Cook for 2 to 3 minutes on each side, or until lightly golden and puffed up.

Meanwhile, peel the onion, then finely chop it along with the apple and toss in a large bowl with a splash of vinegar (this will take the strong raw onion flavor away). Drain and add the tuna, grate over the Cheddar and add the cream cheese. Put a bit of fire in its belly with some English mustard, a pinch of pepper and a shake of Tabasco (if you like), then mix together.

Gently slide the bread from the pan and carefully run the knife all the way around the edge, turning and gradually cutting in towards the middle until you end up with 2 rounds. Slide the top of the bread off, then spread one side with half the filling, pop the top on and push down slightly. Place it back in the pan to cook for 3 to 4 minutes on each side, or until beautifully golden and melty inside. I like to cut these up and share straight away while they're hot – you can be cooking the next one as you tuck into the first.

Portuguese fish stew

My mate Tim Hogg is a massive foodie and wine dude, and has made a life in Portugal that he's so passionate about. He gave me the heads up on this fantastic baked fish stew, which is really interesting because there's no added liquid – everything cooks and steams in its own juices to keep the flavors intense and delicious. I took the liberty of finishing it off under the broiler to crisp up the potatoes, which isn't traditional, but I couldn't help myself.

Serves 4 to 6

Total time: 1 hour 10 minutes

312 calories

2 onions

1 red bell pepper

1 yellow bell pepper

2 medium potatoes

3 ripe tomatoes

olive oil

1 lb white fish fillets, skinned and pin-boned

½ bunch of fresh Italian parsley (½ oz)

1 pinch of dried chili flakes

5 fresh bay leaves

1 loaf of crusty bread, to serve

Using frozen fish works really well in this recipe and helps to get the price down, but see what's available fresh at your fishmonger's first – you might pick up a bargain. The stew can also be embellished with all sorts of exciting and more expensive fish, if you like.

Preheat the oven to 375°F. Peel the onions, seed the peppers (keeping them whole), then take a bit of care to slice them both as finely as you can into rounds on a mandolin (be sure to use the guard!), or by hand with good knife skills. Do the same with the potatoes – I leave the skin on, just give them a scrub – and tomatoes.

Get yourself a wide ovenproof pan (roughly 12 inches in diameter), add the onions and a lug of oil, then fry on a low heat for around 15 minutes, or until soft and sweet, stirring occasionally. Meanwhile, parboil the potatoes in a saucepan of boiling salted water for around 3 minutes, then drain well.

Remove half the onions from the pan, spreading the remaining onion out into a nice layer. Top with a layer of roughly half each of the tomatoes, peppers and potatoes, then cut the fish into ¾-inch slices and layer it all on top. Finely chop the parsley (stalks and all) and sprinkle most of it over the fish with the chili flakes. Drizzle with oil and season lightly, then repeat the veg layers, starting with the remaining onion and finishing with potatoes. Poke in the bay leaves, drizzle with oil and lightly season again. Cover tightly with aluminum foil and bake for 30 minutes, or until the potatoes are cooked through. At this point, I like to remove the foil and place under a hot broiler for 5 minutes, or until the potatoes are golden. Sprinkle over the remaining parsley, and serve with bread to mop up all the lovely juices.

Smoky kipper pâté

Smoked fish pâté is an absolute treat – people seem to go mad for it. I've used kippers in this recipe, but feel free to use smoked trout or hot-smoked salmon instead, if you prefer. Once you've made this it's pretty stable in the fridge for a couple of days, so it's great for dinner parties when you want to get stuff done in advance.

Serves 6

Total time: 30 minutes

287 calories

14 oz smoked kipper fillets

6 slices of ciabatta

14 oz mixed crunchy veg, such as fennel, carrot, beets, English cucumber, little gem lettuce or heart of romaine

2 lemons

½ teaspoon sweet smoked paprika

3 ½ oz reduced-fat cream cheese

1 whole nutmeg, for grating

extra virgin olive oil

Toast or grill the sliced ciabatta until lightly bar-marked. Prep all the veg and cut it into crudité-sized chunks that will be a pleasure to eat.

Place the kippers in a bowl, then scrape away, remove and discard any skin and bigger bones. Put into a food processor (juices and all) along with the zest from 1 lemon, the paprika, cream cheese, a generous pinch of pepper and a good few gratings of nutmeg. Blitz to a consistency of your liking, tweak to your taste with lemon juice, then transfer to a nice serving dish and drizzle with a little oil. Serve with the crunchy veg, toast and the remaining lemon, cut into wedges, for squeezing over.

If you're using smoked trout or hot-smoked salmon, there's no need to cook it – skip straight to the processor bit (discarding the skin) and add a splash of water to loosen, if you think it needs it.

SIMPLE TASTY DISHES

CHEDDAR & PEA OMELET

391 calories

Serves 1
Total time: 15 minutes

Peel and finely chop ½ an onion, then fry it in a non-stick pan on a medium heat with a splash of olive oil for 5 minutes. Add ¾ cup of frozen peas for another 5 minutes, or until softened, stirring regularly. Beat 2 large eggs, quickly stir them into the onions and peas and mix thoroughly, then grate over ¾ oz of Cheddar cheese. Just before the top of the eggs are cooked, fold the omelet in half and slide it onto a plate – the residual heat will finish cooking it through. Eat right away.

LEMON & BASIL SPAGHETTI

582 calories

Serves 1
Total time: 15 minutes

Cook 3 oz of dried spaghetti in a saucepan of boiling salted water according to package instructions. Put the zest and juice of ½ a lemon into a bowl with ½ oz of finely grated Parmesan cheese and 2 tablespoons of olive oil. Pick in the leaves from 2 sprigs of fresh basil. Use tongs to drag the cooked spaghetti into the bowl, adding a little cooking water as needed to loosen and emulsify, then toss really well to melt the cheese and coat the pasta in the sauce. Serve right away, with an extra little grating of Parmesan cheese, if you like.

LESS THAN $2 PER SERVING

MUSHROOMS ON TOAST

160 calories

Serves 1
Total time: 10 minutes

Quarter or slice 3 ½ oz of button mushrooms. Pick a few fresh thyme leaves. Peel and finely slice 1 clove of garlic and put it into a large hot frying pan with 1 teaspoon of unsalted butter. As the garlic starts to lightly color, add the thyme, followed by the mushrooms. Toss around and fry while you toast 1 nice thick slice of bread. Season the mushrooms to perfection, add a splash of water, then pour them straight over the toast. Finish with a few drips of balsamic vinegar, and serve.

SPINACH & ONION QUESADILLA

665 calories

Serves 1
Total time: 10 to 15 minutes

Peel and finely chop ½ an onion and slowly fry it in a pan on a low heat with a drizzle of olive oil for 5 to 10 minutes, or until softened and sweet. Stir in 3 ½ oz of frozen spinach until defrosted and the liquid has evaporated, then season to perfection. Spread the mixture across 1 regular soft flour tortilla, grate over ¾ oz of Cheddar cheese, top with another tortilla and toast in a dry frying pan, turning until golden on both sides. Cut into six wedges and serve with a spoonful of fat-free plain yogurt marbled with a shake of hot chili sauce.

LESS THAN $2 PER SERVING

PAPPA AL POMODORO

224 calories

Serves 2
Total time: 25 minutes

Peel and finely slice 2 cloves of garlic and put into a medium saucepan on a medium heat with a lug of olive oil, the finely chopped stalks from 4 sprigs of fresh basil (save the leaves) and 1 good pinch of dried chili flakes. When lightly golden, add the basil leaves, 2 × 14-oz cans of diced tomatoes and 1 can's worth of water. Bring to a boil and simmer for 5 minutes, then tear in 2 nice slices of stale or lightly toasted bread. Simmer for 10 minutes, season to perfection and serve right away with a drizzle of extra virgin olive oil and a grating of Parmesan cheese, if you like.

CARROT, ORANGE & GINGER SOUP

337 calories

Serves 2
Total time: 35 to 40 minutes

Peel 6 large carrots and 1 onion, roughly chop them and put them into a saucepan on a medium heat with a lug of olive oil, the zest and juice of 1 orange and a ¾-inch piece of peeled and chopped gingerroot. Cook for 15 minutes, stirring occasionally, then remove and mash 2 heaping tablespoons of the mixture on a board. Add 3 cups of boiling water to the pan, bring to a boil and simmer for 15 to 20 minutes, then blitz in a blender until super smooth. Pour back into the pan, season to perfection, and leave to simmer while you toast 2 nice slices of bread and spread them with the smashed carrot mixture. Cut them into soldiers and serve on top of the soup. Shave over ¾ oz of Cheddar cheese and serve.

LEEK & POTATO SOUP

344 calories

Serves 2
Total time: 45 minutes

Wash 2 leeks and peel 1 onion, then roughly chop them and slowly fry in a hot saucepan for 15 minutes with a lug of olive oil and 2 sprigs of fresh thyme, adding a splash of water, if needed, and stirring occasionally. Add 1 peeled and chopped potato and 3 cups of boiling water, then bring to a boil and simmer for 25 minutes, or until the potato is soft. Blitz with an immersion blender until smooth. Season to perfection and keep warm while you poach 2 large eggs to your liking in a saucepan of gently simmering water and toast 2 nice slices of bread. Serve the two together, on top of the soup.

BRITISH CARBONARA

508 calories

Serves 2
Total time: 15 minutes

Cook 5 ½ oz of dried penne in a saucepan of boiling salted water according to package instructions. Slice 4 rashers of smoked bacon and fry in a hot pan with a drizzle of olive oil. When lightly golden, squash in 1 clove of garlic through a garlic press, then add a good pinch of pepper and the leaves from 1 sprig of fresh rosemary and remove from the heat. Beat 1 large egg with 2 oz of finely grated Cheddar cheese, then stir in 4 tablespoons of the pasta cooking water. Drain the pasta, then immediately and thoroughly stir into the bacon pan, followed by the egg mixture, until silky smooth and delicious. If the pan is still sizzling hot, you'll scramble the eggs, so make sure you do this off the heat.

WE ALL LOVE A GOOD FRUIT BOWL . . .

. . . but we don't like it when the fruit gets too ripe too quickly. Don't throw it away – it's got so much potential! Pretty much any fruit can be frozen, either separately or mixed together, kept in plastic containers or sandwich bags. It'll sit there, patiently waiting for you to turn it into any of the delicious ideas below.

FRUIT PREP

Peel bananas and slice them up, pit and chop any stone fruit like mangoes and peaches, core and slice apples and pears, remove the stalks from soft fruit such as berries and give them a quick wash. Squeeze a little lemon juice over any fruit that's prone to discoloring, like apples and pears. Get into the habit of freezing stuff as and when you need to, in whatever quantities you have, helping you to waste less.

SMOOTHIES

Put your frozen fruit combination into a blender, trying always to use half a banana per person to provide body and sweetness. Top up the blender with apple juice or milk, blitz until smooth, then balance the flavor with honey, if needed. Pour into glasses, and serve. Sometimes I like to add a little handful of mild seeds, nuts or even old-fashioned rolled oats, or a dollop of fat-free plain yogurt for a bit of creaminess. A little chunk of fresh peeled gingerroot always works a treat too.

ICE CREAM

For a 1-minute reduced-fat sorbet-cum-ice cream, put equal quantities of frozen fruit and yogurt into a food processor, add a good drizzle of honey and whiz to the consistency of smooth ice cream. Scoop into bowls, glasses, wafers or ice cream cones, or pop it into a pot and put back in the freezer for another time. For me, you can't beat berries here. You can also try using a spoonful of complementary jam to balance the sweetness rather than honey, if you prefer.

LOLLIES

There are two kinds of lollies that I make at home. First, fairly standard juice lollies that we make three or four times a week – we really do make these this often because the kids go wild for them and they've got to be one of the healthiest desserts you can give them. It also takes about 10 minutes for the kids to eat them, which is a good amount of time for their brains to get over that sweet rush of desire. Get some molds off the Internet, fill them with any fresh fruit juice (not from concentrate), pop in a few fresh berries and freeze. Or, second, blend equal quantities of frozen fruit and plain yogurt, loosening with a little milk to help it blend, and sweetening to taste with honey. Pour it back into your large empty yogurt pot, pop in 4 lolly sticks and freeze, then carefully cut into four when ready to eat.

PUDDINGS

Puddings, pies and crumbles are such cheap, easy, delicious desserts to make and absolutely love any single or mixed fruit combinations. You will always need to add sugar to the fruit when stewing to balance acidity and give it that shiny texture, but a handy little trick is to use up any pots of jam that you feel will complement the fruit you've chosen, for example, frozen apple with blackberry jam or frozen blackcurrants with crab-apple jelly instead of sugar. Roughly about 2 heaping tablespoons of jam or sugar per 1 ¼ lbs of fruit will get you to the right place (although sour things like rhubarb and plums may need more of a helping hand).

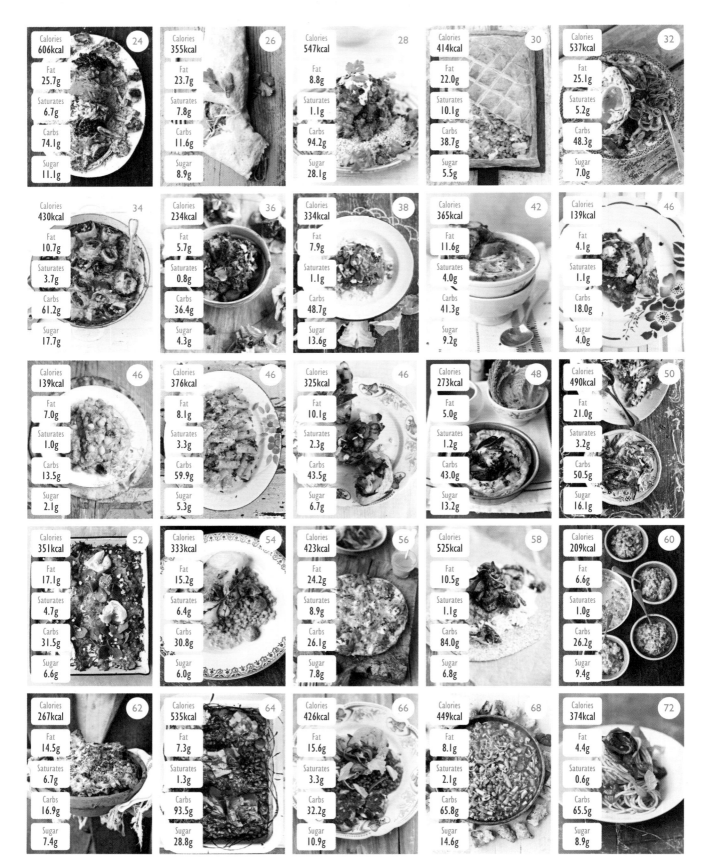

24 Calories 606kcal; Fat 25.7g; Saturates 6.7g; Carbs 74.1g; Sugar 11.1g	**26** Calories 355kcal; Fat 23.7g; Saturates 7.8g; Carbs 11.6g; Sugar 8.9g	**28** Calories 547kcal; Fat 8.8g; Saturates 1.1g; Carbs 94.2g; Sugar 28.1g	**30** Calories 414kcal; Fat 22.0g; Saturates 10.1g; Carbs 38.7g; Sugar 5.5g	**32** Calories 537kcal; Fat 25.1g; Saturates 5.2g; Carbs 48.3g; Sugar 7.0g
34 Calories 430kcal; Fat 10.7g; Saturates 3.7g; Carbs 61.2g; Sugar 17.7g	**36** Calories 234kcal; Fat 5.7g; Saturates 0.8g; Carbs 36.4g; Sugar 4.3g	**38** Calories 334kcal; Fat 7.9g; Saturates 1.1g; Carbs 48.7g; Sugar 13.6g	**42** Calories 365kcal; Fat 11.6g; Saturates 4.0g; Carbs 41.3g; Sugar 9.2g	**46** Calories 139kcal; Fat 4.1g; Saturates 1.1g; Carbs 18.0g; Sugar 4.0g
46 Calories 139kcal; Fat 7.0g; Saturates 1.0g; Carbs 13.5g; Sugar 2.1g	**46** Calories 376kcal; Fat 8.1g; Saturates 3.3g; Carbs 59.9g; Sugar 5.3g	**46** Calories 325kcal; Fat 10.1g; Saturates 2.3g; Carbs 43.5g; Sugar 6.7g	**48** Calories 273kcal; Fat 5.0g; Saturates 1.2g; Carbs 43.0g; Sugar 13.2g	**50** Calories 490kcal; Fat 21.0g; Saturates 3.2g; Carbs 50.5g; Sugar 16.1g
52 Calories 351kcal; Fat 17.1g; Saturates 4.7g; Carbs 31.5g; Sugar 6.6g	**54** Calories 333kcal; Fat 15.2g; Saturates 6.4g; Carbs 30.8g; Sugar 6.0g	**56** Calories 423kcal; Fat 24.2g; Saturates 8.9g; Carbs 26.1g; Sugar 7.8g	**58** Calories 525kcal; Fat 10.5g; Saturates 1.1g; Carbs 84.0g; Sugar 6.8g	**60** Calories 209kcal; Fat 6.6g; Saturates 1.0g; Carbs 26.2g; Sugar 9.4g
62 Calories 267kcal; Fat 14.5g; Saturates 6.7g; Carbs 16.9g; Sugar 7.4g	**64** Calories 535kcal; Fat 7.3g; Saturates 1.3g; Carbs 93.5g; Sugar 28.8g	**66** Calories 426kcal; Fat 15.6g; Saturates 3.3g; Carbs 32.2g; Sugar 10.9g	**68** Calories 449kcal; Fat 8.1g; Saturates 2.1g; Carbs 65.8g; Sugar 14.6g	**72** Calories 374kcal; Fat 4.4g; Saturates 0.6g; Carbs 65.5g; Sugar 8.9g

72 Calories 369kcal · Fat 4.4g · Saturates 0.6g · Carbs 65.5g · Sugar 13.2g	**72** Calories 367kcal · Fat 4.3g · Saturates 0.6g · Carbs 65.4g · Sugar 13.2g	**72** Calories 430kcal · Fat 6.3g · Saturates 0.8g · Carbs 64.0g · Sugar 11.0g	**74** Calories 269kcal · Fat 11g · Saturates 2.4g · Carbs 23.6g · Sugar 4.4g	**78** Calories 643kcal · Fat 22.4g · Saturates 8.2g · Carbs 65.2g · Sugar 15.4g
80 Calories 470kcal · Fat 13.3g · Saturates 3.6g · Carbs 47.8g · Sugar 5.2g	**82** Calories 478kcal · Fat 20.7g · Saturates 3.9g · Carbs 32.6g · Sugar 1.6g	**84** Calories 511kcal · Fat 24.4g · Saturates 12.7g · Carbs 48.4g · Sugar 6.4g	**84** Calories 424kcal · Fat 15.9g · Saturates 7.6g · Carbs 43.3g · Sugar 11.4g	**84** Calories 332kcal · Fat 9.0g · Saturates 3.4g · Carbs 40.5g · Sugar 7.0g
84 Calories 493kcal · Fat 23.3g · Saturates 12.4g · Carbs 47.6g · Sugar 6.4g	**86** Calories 475kcal · Fat 14.3g · Saturates 6.6g · Carbs 70.0g · Sugar 6.4g	**88** Calories 292kcal · Fat 11.0g · Saturates 4.1g · Carbs 29.3g · Sugar 5.9g	**90** Calories 416kcal · Fat 8.9g · Saturates 2.0g · Carbs 52.2g · Sugar 6.3g	**92** Calories 498kcal · Fat 16.3g · Saturates 5.4g · Carbs 55.6g · Sugar 10.6g
96 Calories 893kcal · Fat 26.8g · Saturates 5.7g · Carbs 92.1g · Sugar 26.1g	**98** Calories 543kcal · Fat 14.1g · Saturates 4.3g · Carbs 70.6g · Sugar 8.3g	**100** Calories 340kcal · Fat 13.9g · Saturates 3.2g · Carbs 18.5g · Sugar 15.2g	**102** Calories 608kcal · Fat 14.7g · Saturates 3.7g · Carbs 78.2g · Sugar 18.0g	**104** Calories 622kcal · Fat 11.1g · Saturates 2.4g · Carbs 88.5g · Sugar 12.1g
106 Calories 634kcal · Fat 29.8g · Saturates 7.8g · Carbs 45.6g · Sugar 7.9g	**110** Calories 338kcal · Fat 23.1g · Saturates 6.0g · Carbs 5.5g · Sugar 4.6g	**112** Calories 454kcal · Fat 7.3g · Saturates 1.9g · Carbs 69.2g · Sugar 8.6g	**114** Calories 310kcal · Fat 8.3g · Saturates 1.9g · Carbs 33.8g · Sugar 5.4g	**118** Calories 619kcal · Fat 28.7g · Saturates 9.5g · Carbs 58.3g · Sugar 15.9g

120	122	124	126	126
Calories 563kcal	Calories 485kcal	Calories 427kcal	Calories 714kcal	Calories 596kcal
Fat 20.0g	Fat 16.3g	Fat 22.8g	Fat 22.8g	Fat 24.1g
Saturates 9.8g	Saturates 5.2g	Saturates 6.8g	Saturates 9.3g	Saturates 8.0g
Carbs 64.9g	Carbs 53.2g	Carbs 36.0g	Carbs 63.7g	Carbs 50.5g
Sugar 4.4g	Sugar 14.4g	Sugar 7.4g	Sugar 10.5g	Sugar 9.0g

126	126	128	132	134
Calories 719kcal	Calories 893kcal	Calories 507kcal	Calories 589kcal	Calories 411kcal
Fat 23.3g	Fat 47.7g	Fat 15.5g	Fat 20.7g	Fat 16.8g
Saturates 7.8g	Saturates 23.2g	Saturates 5.6g	Saturates 6.2g	Saturates 5.8g
Carbs 77.9g	Carbs 68.5g	Carbs 66.7g	Carbs 64.7g	Carbs 34.3g
Sugar 10.0g	Sugar 9.3g	Sugar 5.5g	Sugar 6.0g	Sugar 3.4g

138	140	142	144	146
Calories 327kcal	Calories 628kcal	Calories 559kcal	Calories 465kcal	Calories 563kcal
Fat 14.0g	Fat 41.5g	Fat 26.6g	Fat 9.7g	Fat 27.6g
Saturates 4.0g	Saturates 21.3g	Saturates 11.7g	Saturates 2.9g	Saturates 10.3g
Carbs 15.5g	Carbs 34.7g	Carbs 49.9g	Carbs 69.3g	Carbs 41.9g
Sugar 7.2g	Sugar 6.9g	Sugar 10.2g	Sugar 4.6g	Sugar 10.0g

150	152	156	160	162
Calories 549kcal	Calories 284kcal	Calories 417kcal	Calories 664kcal	Calories 473kcal
Fat 26.9g	Fat 20.7g	Fat 20.9g	Fat 15.7g	Fat 11.6g
Saturates 9.2g	Saturates 6.7g	Saturates 5.9g	Saturates 5.8g	Saturates 2.7g
Carbs 39.6g	Carbs 5.4g	Carbs 24.9g	Carbs 92.8g	Carbs 54.3g
Sugar 6.4g	Sugar 5.2g	Sugar 19.6g	Sugar 5.2g	Sugar 18.0g

164	166	168	170	172
Calories 323kcal	Calories 174kcal	Calories 395kcal	Calories 442kcal	Calories 613kcal
Fat 5.2g	Fat 5.2g	Fat 13.1g	Fat 17.6g	Fat 20.1g
Saturates 1.5g	Saturates 1.2g	Saturates 4.4g	Saturates 5.8g	Saturates 7.9g
Carbs 47.5g	Carbs 12.8g	Carbs 39.2g	Carbs 38.7g	Carbs 65.5g
Sugar 5.1g	Sugar 10.0g	Sugar 5.2g	Sugar 14.3g	Sugar 5.4g

Calories 782kcal 174	Calories 592kcal 178	Calories 583kcal 180	Calories 670kcal 182	Calories 744kcal 186
Fat 42.0g	Fat 17.0g	Fat 38.1g	Fat 54.1g	Fat 40.2g
Saturates 14.7g	Saturates 5.8g	Saturates 8.7g	Saturates 18.7g	Saturates 13.4g
Carbs 35.8g	Carbs 73.4g	Carbs 39.0g	Carbs 19.2g	Carbs 61.3g
Sugar 32.7g	Sugar 12.6g	Sugar 14.4g	Sugar 10.3g	Sugar 15.7g

Calories 693kcal 188	Calories 664kcal 194	Calories 778kcal 196	Calories 297kcal 198	Calories 473kcal 200
Fat 14.6g	Fat 25.4g	Fat 18.2g	Fat 7.0g	Fat 24.3g
Saturates 5.2g	Saturates 9.9g	Saturates 7.1g	Saturates 1.9g	Saturates 4.7g
Carbs 55.4g	Carbs 62.6g	Carbs 101.5g	Carbs 36.9g	Carbs 43.3g
Sugar 17.8g	Sugar 13.2g	Sugar 7.3g	Sugar 7.1g	Sugar 4.9g

Calories 360kcal 202	Calories 540kcal 204	Calories 462kcal 206	Calories 472kcal 210	Calories 492kcal 212
Fat 16.9g	Fat 18.8g	Fat 12.3g	Fat 19.9g	Fat 21.8g
Saturates 6.9g	Saturates 6.7g	Saturates 2.7g	Saturates 7.0g	Saturates 10.3g
Carbs 27.5g	Carbs 62.2g	Carbs 61.5g	Carbs 42.2g	Carbs 40.4g
Sugar 5.3g	Sugar 18.0g	Sugar 5.9g	Sugar 13.8g	Sugar 10.7g

Calories 478kcal 214	Calories 495kcal 218	Calories 393kcal 220	Calories 393kcal 224	Calories 358kcal 224
Fat 16.3g	Fat 22.3g	Fat 18.9g	Fat 25.9g	Fat 13.0g
Saturates 5.5g	Saturates 4.5g	Saturates 3.3g	Saturates 8.7g	Saturates 4.1g
Carbs 49.4g	Carbs 32.8g	Carbs 33.6g	Carbs 18.1g	Carbs 36.8g
Sugar 5.9g	Sugar 5.5g	Sugar 3.7g	Sugar 1.1g	Sugar 4.2g

Calories 334kcal 224	Calories 537kcal 224	Calories 449kcal 226	Calories 458kcal 228	Calories 398kcal 230
Fat 10.6g	Fat 19.4g	Fat 24.2g	Fat 24.0g	Fat 13.8g
Saturates 2.6g	Saturates 6.5g	Saturates 6.1g	Saturates 3.7g	Saturates 3.0g
Carbs 32.5g	Carbs 54.5g	Carbs 34.3g	Carbs 32.7g	Carbs 37.9g
Sugar 1.4g	Sugar 3.0g	Sugar 5.2g	Sugar 12.9g	Sugar 9.0g

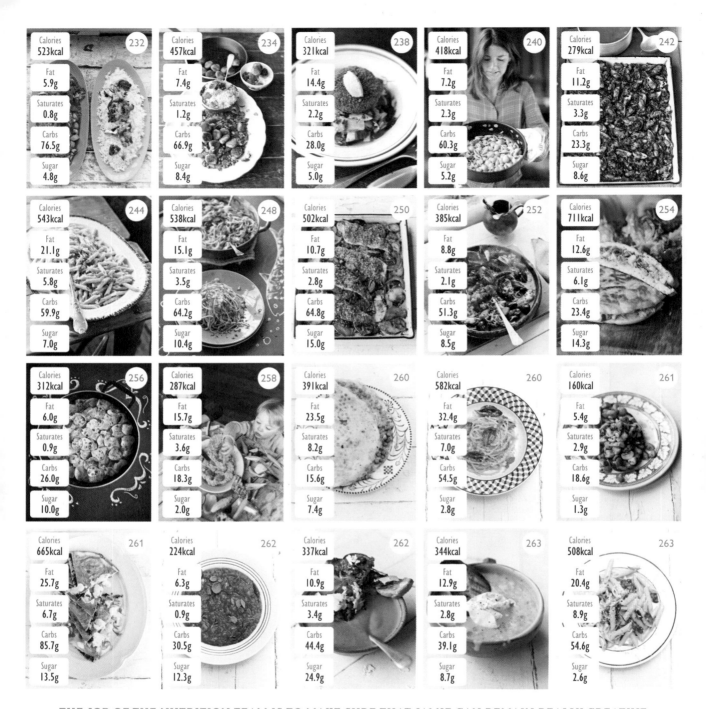

Calories 523kcal · Fat 5.9g · Saturates 0.8g · Carbs 76.5g · Sugar 4.8g — 232

Calories 457kcal · Fat 7.4g · Saturates 1.2g · Carbs 66.9g · Sugar 8.4g — 234

Calories 321kcal · Fat 14.4g · Saturates 2.2g · Carbs 28.0g · Sugar 5.0g — 238

Calories 418kcal · Fat 7.2g · Saturates 2.3g · Carbs 60.3g · Sugar 5.2g — 240

Calories 279kcal · Fat 11.2g · Saturates 3.3g · Carbs 23.3g · Sugar 8.6g — 242

Calories 543kcal · Fat 21.1g · Saturates 5.8g · Carbs 59.9g · Sugar 7.0g — 244

Calories 538kcal · Fat 15.1g · Saturates 3.5g · Carbs 64.2g · Sugar 10.4g — 248

Calories 502kcal · Fat 10.7g · Saturates 2.8g · Carbs 64.8g · Sugar 15.0g — 250

Calories 385kcal · Fat 8.8g · Saturates 2.1g · Carbs 51.3g · Sugar 8.5g — 252

Calories 711kcal · Fat 12.6g · Saturates 6.1g · Carbs 23.4g · Sugar 14.3g — 254

Calories 312kcal · Fat 6.0g · Saturates 0.9g · Carbs 26.0g · Sugar 10.0g — 256

Calories 287kcal · Fat 15.7g · Saturates 3.6g · Carbs 18.3g · Sugar 2.0g — 258

Calories 391kcal · Fat 23.5g · Saturates 8.2g · Carbs 15.6g · Sugar 7.4g — 260

Calories 582kcal · Fat 32.4g · Saturates 7.0g · Carbs 54.5g · Sugar 2.8g — 260

Calories 160kcal · Fat 5.4g · Saturates 2.9g · Carbs 18.6g · Sugar 1.3g — 261

Calories 665kcal · Fat 25.7g · Saturates 6.7g · Carbs 85.7g · Sugar 13.5g — 261

Calories 224kcal · Fat 6.3g · Saturates 0.9g · Carbs 30.5g · Sugar 12.3g — 262

Calories 337kcal · Fat 10.9g · Saturates 3.4g · Carbs 44.4g · Sugar 24.9g — 262

Calories 344kcal · Fat 12.9g · Saturates 2.8g · Carbs 39.1g · Sugar 8.7g — 263

Calories 508kcal · Fat 20.4g · Saturates 8.9g · Carbs 54.6g · Sugar 2.6g — 263

THE JOB OF THE NUTRITION TEAM IS TO MAKE SURE THAT JAMIE CAN REMAIN REALLY CREATIVE WITH HIS RECIPE WRITING, BUT ENSURE THAT A LOT OF THE RECIPES ARE HEALTHY TOO.

The nutrition information printed in the book is based on established theoretical data. The nutrient values may vary from those published. Serving sizes are based on recipe recommendations, unless otherwise specified, and will generally not include extras of unspecified quantity, for example: "fat-free plain yogurt, to serve." In this book we have set specific nutrition targets to classify a recipe as "healthy." For example, a healthy main meal would consist of less than 35 percent of a woman's RDI (recommended daily intake) or DV (daily value) for calories and saturated fat, and less than 25 percent RDI or DV for salt, assuming people are seasoning in moderation (based on North American guidelines). Recipes for side dishes, starters and soups have their own nutrition targets. Where possible the recipes are balanced meals containing each of the food groups. Remember that a healthy balanced diet and regular exercise are the keys to a healthy lifestyle.

LAURA PARR — JAMIE'S HEAD NUTRITIONIST

FIND OUT MORE

For more nutritional advice, as well as videos, features, lots of handy hints, tips and tricks on all sorts of different subjects, and loads of fantastic, tasty recipes, plus much more, make sure you check out jamieoliver.com and jamieshomecookingskills.com.

If you want a hands-on cooking experience and more thrifty advice, see if there's a Jamie's Ministry of Food center near you. All the lovely staff have great knowledge and real experience – visit jamiesministryoffood.com to find out more.

JAMIEOLIVER.COM

CLARE PARKER

OUR THRIFTY LUNCHERS
VAL McARTHUR
NIKKI CRICHTON
MEALTA ROBINSON
SIMON CLARK

JULIETTE BUTLER

CHRISTINA MACKENZIE

ANNIE LEE

MADDIE RIX

BARNABY PURDY

GEORGINA HAYDEN

DAVID LOFTUS

REBECCA WALKER

LAURA JAMES

KATE BURTON

T

H

A

ANSA KHAN KHATTAK

JAY HUNT
&
NICK HORNBY
AT CHANNEL 4

LOUISE MOORE

BOBBY SEBIRE

PETE BEGG

EMILY KENNEDY

CHARLIE CLAPP

KATIE MILLARD

ABIGAIL FAWCETT

JO LORD

AMELIA CROOK

MIKE MATTHEWS

ALL MY WONDERFUL OFFICE TESTERS

HELEN MARTIN

BECCA SULOCKI

ZOE COLLINS

LOUISA JAMES

JAMES VERITY

BETHAN O'CONNOR

RACHEL YOUNG

JOHN HAMILTON

GINNY ROLFE

TOM WELDON

ELIZABETH SMITH

NICK POPE

HOLLY ADAMS

ALLY BRIGHT

SARAH TILDESLEY

ROZZIE BATCHELAR

NICK LOWNDES

OUR THRIFTY LUNCHERS
LAURA FLEMING
ANDIE LAIDLAW
SUSAN SPENCE
JO GILDER

PHILLIPPA SPENCE

JO RALLING

CHANTAL NOEL

ISABEL HAYMAN-BROWN

TARA DONOVAN

CATHERINE WOOD

LOUISE HOLLAND

HANNAH BRADBURY

JODENE JORDAN

MATT RUSSELL

SAM BALDWIN

EMILY WOOD

MY LOVELY FAMILY

SIMON COLLINS

ELLA TAYLOR

EMILIE SPENCER

JOHN STENTON

CLAIRE FAGAN

ROB CARTER

TAMSIN ENGLISH

CLAIRE POSTANS

LUCY BERESFORD-KNOX

SIMON WEEKES

T

H

A

FABIAN PONTON
KELLIE ROWBOTHAM
KEITH WARDLEY

KATH TIBBALS

GIOVANNA MILIA

MALOU HERKES

EMI CHIAPPA

NAOMI FIDLER

JACK O'SHEA

ROSANGELA AMADEI

JOHN LEAVEY & TONY BOOTH

MIKE SARAH

DANIEL NOWLAND

AYSSA & THE ONLINE TEAM

EMMA WHITE

SEAN MOXHAY

JOE SARAH

LIMA O'DONNELL

THERESE MacDERMOTT

GEORGE RIAD

CHARLIE PHILLIPS
GEORGE FIDDES

JULIE AKEROYD

LAURA PARR

LUKE CARDIFF

JULIA BELL

MARK ARN

JOE YULE

N

K

S

JOHN JACKSON

ALL THE HARD-WORKING GANG AT THE OFFICE

HELEN PRATT

PETER BERRY

ANNA DERKACZ

AMBER SAYER

CRISPIN FORSTER

CAROLINE WILDING

DEBBIE HATFIELD
PAT RUSH
CAROLINE PRETTY

JONNY GARRETT

DAN EASTWOOD

CALUM THOMSON

BEN SHAUGNESSY

TAYLOR RICHARDSON

GUDREN CLAIRE

PATRICIO & THE IT TEAM

STUART ANDERSON

INDEX

Recipes marked V are suitable for vegetarians
Recipes marked L use leftovers

C
....